I0415553

GOOD TO GO

Your pocket guide to US Navy boot camp

by A.N. Kindig

Copyright © 2012 Alexis N. Kindig.
All rights reserved.

ISBN: 978 – 1 – 105 – 89594 – 4

To my parents, for everything.
And to my brother, for other things.

Contents

Introduction

Firstly, I would like to congratulate you on your decision to join the United States Navy. You've heard it before, but it's true; this is a major step in a lot of ways, and you should take advantage of all the resources and unique opportunities available to you as a Sailor. As a member of the fleet, you'll have the chance to advance yourself personally and professionally, to learn a lot, both academically and in terms of life experience, and to go places and do things most people don't.

For now, though, you're a Future Sailor with a lot of questions and with a major initiatory experience looming on your horizon. I was standing in your shoes myself not too long ago, and I wished I had had access to better, more complete and more accurate information before I shipped out for boot camp. There is an online book about boot camp out there, and some information floating around the Internet; I read it, and it was better than nothing, but it left a lot of territory uncovered and some of it wasn't particularly accurate. I was also fortunate to have a great recruiter, who answered my questions as best he could and never steered me wrong. And yet, even with the information available to me, there was still something missing. All the information I read told about some general things that would happen, but did not mention the kinds of skills or traits you should already have before you go, nor did they go into detail about daily life. And recruiters perhaps aren't encouraged to tell the full truth about the emotional and physical impacts of boot camp. They're more likely to tell you it's easy and that nothing bad will happen. It's certainly unlikely that you will have a miserable time or get seriously injured, but boot camp is not all sweetness and light. There are major adjustments to be made and it's not always easy to make them.

Therefore, this book aims to meet two goals: one; to give you details on the kinds of things you really want and need to know, and two; to give you the truth of boot camp, both the good and the bad. Your experience will not be precisely as described in the following chapters, but if you encounter any major surprises at boot camp, I haven't done my job.

I'm not going to tell you that this book is some kind of golden ticket that will guarantee that you will breeze through your basic training without so much as a bump. No book or product or piece of advice will do that. Boot camp is designed to shake you up, make you lose your individuality for a while and put you in situations you wouldn't normally choose to be in. But, this book will give you good advice and will give you all the details I think I would like to have known going in.

As you read this book, keep in mind that your boot camp experience will be unique to you. The boot camp curriculum is presented in a very specific and regimented way, so the details outlined in this book will be similar for everyone, but there are exceptions to just about any situation. The things I detail in this book are true for the majority of Recruits, but I cannot guarantee that your boot camp experience will be exactly as laid out here. I can say with confidence, however, that the information in this book will arm you for life at boot camp and provide you with a more accurate picture than other sources. Whether your boot camp experience is largely positive, largely negative or just ho-hum depends on your attitude, the people around you, and a little dumb luck. The bulk of this book addresses the things that a normal, well-adjusted Recruit can expect from a normal boot camp situation.

It is possible to get kicked out of boot camp. It is possible to get hurt, or get sick or get set back to a later graduation date. These are exceptions. The possibility of these things happening shouldn't worry you. Most of these situations are avoidable through the use of common sense and caution on your part.

There is a moment (or perhaps a few moments) in boot camp when every Recruit asks him- or herself, "What was I thinking? Why did I want to do this?" It's just a moment. It will pass. You have not made a bad decision. Boot camp is its own strange little world, with strange rules and ways of doing things. The real Navy is not like boot camp. Once you get out of boot camp, you will find that you are treated like a person, an individual. You will lose the fear and trembling instilled in you throughout your time at Great Lakes.

I would not describe boot camp as easy, but neither is it particularly difficult. The most difficult fight you will have is with yourself as you let go of your ego, get used to being away from home, and put up with things that irritate you. It is my hope that this book will arm you with knowledge that will allow you to get through basic training with a positive attitude. We fear most that which we don't understand; I believe that if you can go to Great Lakes with a good idea of what you can expect, your anxiety will be minimized and your daily life will be a little easier.

If I sometimes sound a little preachy during the course of this book, I apologize in advance. However, if I do preach it's because I'm trying to emphasize points that I know from experience are important. If I repeat myself a lot or sound high-handed, it's because I'm talking about a point I believe strongly you should take to heart.

So, here's to you, shipmate. The ball is in your court now. I hope that your time at boot camp provides you with some good stories to tell afterwards and a few good times along the way. There is one major similarity between boot camp and the Navy at large, and that is that you will find yourself in the company of all kinds of people from all over the country, and even all over the world. I'm still in contact with many of the people from my division, and I have a lot of good (or at least amusing) memories. I hope the same will be true for you.

NOTE: words that have been **bolded like this** are in the glossary at the end of the book.

Before You Go

As I've said, your boot camp experience will be unique to you. Even so, there are certain things you can go in with that will make your life at Great Lakes much easier. This section is dedicated to detailing some of the main things you can do or know before-hand that will greatly benefit you.

Get in shape. From my experience, one big mis-take people make going in is not taking the physi-cal requirements of boot camp seriously. Now, the Navy's expectations of your physical fitness level are perfectly reasonable. A young, decently fit person should not have a problem meeting or even exceed-ing the requirements. And yet, there are plenty of Recruits who struggle with the physical aspects, especially running. There will almost certainly be three or four people in your division who puke when running laps and don't pass their PFAs (Physical Fitness Assessments) because of poor run times. You don't have to be one of those people.

If you aren't already jogging every day, START NOW. You don't need to be a superstar runner, but for a non-runner, it can take a long time to become proficient. For your PFA, you will need to run a mile and a half. If you cannot now run that distance with-out stopping or walking, you have work to do. It's far better to get that work done now than at boot camp, when you may simply not have the time to build up the speed or endurance you will need to pass your final run. I cannot overemphasize this: get consistently good at running a mile and a half before you go. You will suffer needlessly otherwise.

The rest of the PFA consists of push-ups and sit-ups. (For a chart of requirements, see the section on the PFA). Again, it's best to make sure you can do the required amount before you go. However, if you are still struggling with these things when you arrive at Great Lakes, they are easier to become better at than running is. You will probably find that you become better at them just from doing them during the course of normal physical training (PT).

It is also very wise to learn how to swim before you ship out, but more on that later.

Again, the physical requirements are not unreasonable, but they are also nothing to sneeze at. Inability to pass regular fitness tests is a major reason for separation from the Navy, both in boot camp and in the fleet.

Get the right attitude. Never underestimate the power of your own attitude. Your mindset can make or break you in boot camp. The advice I am about to give you is the single most important advice in this entire book. If you forget everything else you read in this book, at least remember this section.

Boot camp is a mental game. As important as it is to be able to meet the physical requirements, your mentality will make the difference between whether you are miserable at boot camp or get through it pretty easily. Your RDCs are masters of the mental game. They know ways of shaking up even the most even-keeled of Recruits. They are also skilled at measuring your response to these tricks. So, if they get in your face or get under your skin and you freeze up or get mad or start to cry, they'll work at you even harder. On the the other hand, if they see that you don't get overly flustered and that you take things in stride and listen to the lesson they're trying to impart, they'll be done with you much quicker. If you have a thin skin or tend to take things personally, be prepared for a bumpy ride at boot camp. You really need to get into a mental attitude where you can let things roll off your back.

This is not to say that you shouldn't take boot camp seriously. You should. Just don't make a bigger deal of things than they really are. Take criticism and punishment in stride. Everyone gets yelled at for something, eventually. It's not personal. It might feel personal, but it isn't. It's just the Great Lakes method of teaching.

Boot camp is run the way it is because it works. Great Lakes has one goal; to make you into a basically trained Sailor. Boot camp is a strange world and a lot of things don't make a whole lot of sense on the surface, but there is a reason for all of it. Everything is done for the purpose of making you ready for the fleet. You may not be able to see it at the the time, but when you look back at your boot camp experience, you'll realize just how deliberate it all was. Attention to detail, military bearing and obedience to orders are the main lessons, and everything you do is geared toward those goals.

In a nutshell: be mature, be cooperative, don't take things harder than you need to and remember that it'll be over in a few weeks. Roll with the punches. Lose the notion that the things you do should have an obvious purpose. Be ready to deal with frustration, boredom and irritation. Leave your ego at home.

And one more thing: Live in the moment. Don't think too far ahead. Life at boot camp is just a series of tasks to be performed. Deal with each task as it comes up and focus totally on it. Then move on to the next one. The days move much faster when you break them up in your mind like that, plus you'll find that your attention to detail improves when you're not dwelling on what's going to happen tomorrow or next week or later this afternoon.

Rank recognition, the Sailor's Creed, and the Eleven General Orders. If you don't know what these three things are, you'll want to talk to your recruiter right away because he's falling down on the job. I'm not going to waste paper and ink or the space in your e-reader by including these things in the book, because your recruiter should already have provided you a booklet with them in it, and if he hasn't, you should ask him for one as soon as possible.

You should start studying rank recognition because you'll need to know who's who at boot camp right off the bat. If you call a petty officer a chief you'll get corrected in a probably not-so-nice manner, and God forbid you call a chief a petty officer. They really hate that. There are also senior chiefs and master chiefs lurking around, and a few officers, and you do not want to make a mistake when addressing them. If you're reasonably comfortable with rank recognition going in, you'll be at a definite advantage. You might even earn yourself a few brownie points your first day.

The Sailor's Creed and the Eleven General Orders of a Sentry are important because you will be called on to know them by heart within the first week or two of boot camp. You can be asked any general order at any time by anyone. It's not unheard-of for Recruits to be asked to recite a general order or the Creed on their first day. It's best to be prepared.

You will also need to know the Chain of Command, which starts with the President and runs all the way down to your RDCs. Because this changes periodically, and because some of it will be specific to your division, I will not include that, either, but you can give yourself a head start by knowing who the President, Secretary of Defense, and Secretary of the Navy currently are.

You will also be called on to memorize the RTC Maxim, which is simply, "I will not lie, cheat, or steal, nor tolerate those among us who do."

There are some recommendations floating around the Internet that you know how to fold 45° folds in your sheets, how to perform facing movements and how to march, how to iron shirts and pants, and the proper way to fold all the clothes you will receive. I'm advising you to not waste your time on those things. You will not be at any disadvantage if you do not know these things going in. You will be thoroughly trained in all this along with everyone else (except for how to iron shirts and pants, since the Navy doesn't even use the uniform that requires that anymore).

What to take with you. Everyone wants to know what's okay to take, and there are different lists floating around the Internet and maybe even around your local recruiting office. Here's the straight, correct answer; don't take anything other than the clothes you're wearing and the following items:

- A small address book with loved ones' numbers and addresses

- A phone card
- A little bit of money, for the airports
- Your social security card and ID
- A blank check (you'll need it when you sign up for the mandatory direct deposit program)
- Your cell phone (you'll have to send it home, but it's good to have for the airports and you can use it for your 30-second call home once you get there)
- A small religious medallion, if you're so inclined

Wear a watch if you normally wear one. You might be allowed to keep it, though you won't be able to wear it. It's kind of nice to have it in your personal drawer, though, so you can wear it on liberty weekend. You can also take some stamps if you like, but you will be provided with stamps and stationery when you get there, so it's not really necessary.

That's it. Don't take anything else; not a pack of Kleenex, not Chapstick, not a hairbrush, not lotion, not your expensive running shoes, not extra underwear, not a snack for later, nothing. Just the clothes on your back and whatever paperwork you were given by your recruiter or at MEPS. Anything else that you take will either go in the trash or be shipped home at your expense. So don't spend money on stuff you think you might need before you go, and tell your family not to give you anything to take (except maybe a phone card or a little cash). And don't try to sneak stuff past the petty officers; whatever you keep that you were told to get rid of is considered contraband, and it will be found eventually and you will be sorry.

The Facilities

Recruit Training Command. Great Lakes is really two bases; the Recruit Training Command (RTC) and the "regular" base, which is home to several A-schools. For our purposes, we'll focus on Recruit Training Command, otherwise known as boot camp.

RTC is a big place with buildings that tend to be in clusters with lots of open space in between. The facilities are divided between three "camps;" Camp John Paul Jones, Camp Porter and Camp Moffett. The processing and main administrative buildings are in Camp Moffett; Camp Porter holds barracks, the gym, the chapel, several trainers and two drill halls; and Camp John Paul Jones is mainly barracks. You'll be doing quite a bit of marching back and forth between the camps.

The admin buildings in Camp Moffett are pretty old, but the barracks are all fairly new and in good shape. Each barracks (known as a "ship," see p. 15) has its own **galley** and classrooms.

A Word on "Ships"

All the buildings at boot camp, including the barracks, are named after famous Naval ships. The new arrival barracks are the USS *Pearl Harbor*; the pool is the USS *Arizona*, etc. The buildings, therefore, are not generally referred to as buildings. They're called ships. Thus, if someone asks you, "What ship are you are in?" they're asking where you are berthed. You would say, "The *Reuben James*," or "The *Bonhomme Richard*," or whatever. Each barracks also has a number, which you'll need to know for the purposes of signing in and out if you're going somewhere on your own.

Life at boot camp makes a little more sense if you actually pretend that you're living on a ship. Using Naval jargon and doing things like standing watch and sticking close to the wall when you walk down the **P-way** fall into place a little easier if you see them in terms of shipboard life.

Compartments. You will live in a room called a compartment, because that is what rooms in ships are called. This is basically just a big rectangular room with a couple of tables and some chairs (which you won't sit on) in the middle, racks (bunk beds) around the edges, a laundry room in the corner, a **head** and a small supply closet on one side and an office, usually called a "fish tank" or "shark tank," in another corner.

Much of your daily life will center around the compartment. This is, of course, where you will sleep and **hygiene**, and there is also quite a bit of instruction and other activities that take place here. All inspections, other than drill inspection, also take place in the compartment. In short, the compartment will be your home during your stay at boot camp.

Your division will actually be spread across two compartments, which you will share with another division. For example, the females in my division shared a compartment with the females from Division 908, and our males shared with their males. Despite the fact that the compartments are shared, one compartment will be considered "yours" and the other will belong to the other division. Our division "owned" the male compartment, so when we had to do something together as a division, we females would go across the P-way. When 908 got together, their males would come over to our side.

There's more on racks and showers in another section, but here's a brief overview. The racks are bunk beds. There are no ladders up to the top bunks; the people on top have to step on the rack below to get up and down. The beds flip up to reveal a locker underneath. This is where you'll keep most of your gear. There are also hooks on the racks for coats, hats and sweatsuits.

The head has three components: sinks, toilets and showers. Upon walking in, you'll see a row of sinks on a wall. Behind that, there is a row of toilets and a few urinals. The toilets are all in separate cubicles with curtains across the front, which is a nice concession to privacy. There is one big shower and a smaller shower. The big shower has two water pillars, and the smaller has one. There is no privacy in the showers.

You and the division you are berthed with will be responsible for keeping the compartments clean. You'll probably need to sweep up the dust bunnies on a daily basis, and the head will need to be neat and dry at all times.

There are windows in the compartments, but they're opaque so you can't see out and sealed so you can't jump or escape. Not that you'd try.

⚓

Arrival

Ah, there is nothing quite like the anxiety and uncertainty of your first hours of boot camp. Being in a strange place, having strangers yelling at you and the distinct feeling that perhaps you've made a mistake in enlisting all add up to a rather nerve-wracking experience. However, by giving you a walk-through of the arrival process, perhaps I can help allay just a little bit of that anxiety for you.

I think the best way to go about this is to relate my experience to you. I arrived at the airport pretty late at night. There were four or five other Recruits on the plane with me, and we all made our way to the aiport's USO (which was pretty difficult to find). At the USO, we handed our packets to an RTC representative and waited while he did whatever he needed to do with them. Then, a petty officer rounded us up and took us all down to an open area to await the bus.

It was abundantly clear even at this point that these guys weren't messing around. We were told to throw away any toiletries we had with us; a lot of us had brought some, like toothpaste, lotion, whatever. Don't bring that stuff; it just ends up in a big trash can at the airport. We were then made to separate into male and female groups and sit cross-legged on the airport floor, in silence.

The bus finally arrived and we all filed on. We had been allowed to buy bottled water at the airport and were advised to drink it all on the bus, because you are going to have to pee in a cup when you get to Great Lakes. The bus ride took maybe forty-five minutes or so, and we were shown a video while we rode about life at boot camp.

Upon arrival, new Recruits enter the in-processing building, known as Golden Thirteen. As soon as we got in the door, the orders and the name-calling started. It is important to note that there are tile flags all over the passageway floors in Golden Thirteen. Please, for your own sake, do not step on these flags.

We were told to get our cell phones out and make our phone calls. You get about thirty seconds to tell someone back home that you have arrived. Basically it's, "Hi, I'm here, I'm okay, bye."

The next step was to go into a room with little desks and fill out some paperwork. I don't remember exactly what was on there, but it was stuff like "What do you expect to get out of the Navy?" and things like that. We were also given a pen and a notebook and told to start writing down the chain of command (it's on a poster on the wall). This is all basically busy work while you wait until you have to pee and while your files are taken care of. Then, it was time for the pee test. You get your little cup and your little bottle and go into the head. There will be someone watching you pee. There are no stalls, just a row of toilets. Once I'd provided my sample, I went out and joined the line for turning in the cup. While you wait, you'll be holding your cup of pee up over your shoulder so they can see you're not tampering with it. You give your name and social security number and they make sure your sample gets properly marked. It was at this point that I first heard someone get called a "fucking retard;" he didn't know his Social Security number.

After the pee test, I got weighed and measured and had my feet measured for shoes. The Navy has these machines that you stand on and they analyze your feet and then tell you what size and type of shoe you need. You must remember this information so you can tell the shoe issuer what you need.

We were given sweatsuits and told to change in the head (more on this below). Then the rest of the night and early morning were spent getting an initial gear issue and packing our boxes to send home.

There are petty officers everywhere in Golden Thirteen and they will be watching you like hawks. They like to start the intimidation and personal insults early on so you don't get out of hand later.

We were also lined up against the wall so someone from the barbershop could check out our hair and determine if we needed haircuts. I deliberately got my hair cut to just above collar length a couple of days before I shipped out. Guess what? They frickin' cut it anyway. More on haircuts below.

All of this takes several hours. There's a lot to get done and a lot of gear to issue, especially if you're there during the winter (things like ski masks, watch caps and two pairs of gloves are standard issue in the winter months). And of course, all this can only take place at the pace of the slowest Recruit, so there's a lot of hurry up and wait. When it's all over and you've sent out your box and stuffed your seabag full of gear, you'll probably be pretty tired and a little overwhelmed. Just so you know, among the gear you will receive is:

- A sewing kit
- Pens and sharpies
- Nail clippers
- Toiletries (bodywash, shaving cream, razors, etc.)
- Shower shoes
- A stamp kit
- A bathing suit
- **Skivvies** (and bras for the ladies)
- A lock for your personal drawer
- A bag of tube socks
- A Recruit ball cap
- A Trainee Guide

- A copy of the latest edition of *The Bluejacket's Manual*
- A Recruit card with something like $150 on it. Works like a debit card or gift card, for use at the NEX and the barber.

All this gear will go inside a sea bag, which is a giant green duffel bag that you wear like a backpack. By the way, even though this stuff is standard issue, it isn't free. The cost of all this gear, plus the price of the uniforms you receive at boot camp, will be deducted from your pay check.

Later on comes what they call the "Moment of Truth." This is when they cram a bunch of new arrivals into a classroom and someone in charge comes in and yells at you. In my case, it was a master chief. The purpose of the Moment of Truth is to scare you into revealing any secrets you may have been keeping. I shouldn't have to say this, but I will: It's a very bad idea to keep secrets from the Navy. Even if they don't find out anyway, most likely whatever it is you're hiding is going to come out eventually, and then the consequences will be even worse than if you had just been honest in the first place. I'm not talking about things like, "I broke my toe when I was eleven and didn't put it on my medical record," or "I smoked weed once when I was sixteen." I'm talking about things like, "I have a heart condition but I don't think it's a big deal and I really want to be a Sailor, so I haven't said anything," or "I'm a drug dealer." We probably all have some details we haven't told our recruiters about. Again, the master chief doesn't need to hear your weepy confession about the fender-bender you caused. He wants to hear about the major stuff, like criminal records or chronic medical conditions. Don't get freaked out into spilling every detail of your past life. On the other hand, if you're feeling guilty during the Moment of Truth, there may be a reason for that.

My division finally assembled in a classroom early the next morning and met our three RDCs. They talked to us for a couple of hours, took us over to the adjacent building, the *Pearl Harbor*, for breakfast, and then marched us over to our ship. Now, I didn't know this at the time, but that is apparently somewhat unusual. Most divisions, I have since learned, spend at least one night in temporary berthing in the *Pearl Harbor*. This is usually where RDCs come to pick up their divisions. I'm not sure why my division was different, but be prepared for either outcome.

It was a long slog in very cold weather to our ship, and once we got there we spent the rest of the day and most of the evening labeling everything in our seabags. Some items get stamped with your stamp kit, others get initialed with your Sharpie.

Each item is done in a very particular way, so pay close attention here.

That night, we were allowed to go to bed at 2000, since most of us hadn't slept in over 24 hours by that point. We were also allowed to sleep until 0800 the next morning, which was the last time that ever happened. This may not happen for you; it just depends on how nice your RDCs are.

That first day will be a very, very long day. Most Recruits arrive at night and are kept awake and busy until the next night, so you will most likely be exhausted by the end of your first day. You can expect some moments of awkwardness and discomfort (like peeing or undressing in front of several people or seeing your new haircut for the first time), but the main tricks to surviving that first day unscathed are just to pay attention, be respectful, and accomplish your tasks quickly and accurately. Oh, and don't fall asleep.

A Word on Language

I had heard somewhere that the RDCs at boot camp are no longer allowed to cuss at you or call you names. I don't remember the source of that information, but it was *wrong*.

I have never heard such constant and creative use of foul language as I heard at RTC. It started the moment we entered Golden Thirteen and didn't stop for two months. At first, it was a bit shocking, but I quickly got used to it, and even began to appreciate just how many different uses there are for the F-word. It has to be the most versatile word in the English language.

In addition to curse words of all degree, there is also a certain amount of name-calling, mild personal insults, and threats of violence (which aren't carried out). Here is a short list of some of the things you may be expect to be called: shitbag; retard; dumbass; fucker; nasty-ass; motherfucker; asshole; ass-clown. And the list goes on. It just depends on how creative the person addressing you is and what mood they're in.

If you have a last name any more unusual than Smith or Jones, be prepared to have it deliberately mispronounced. And if your name might conceivably be altered to resemble a sexual term or curse word, well, that will probably be your new name. You may also be given a nickname based on physical appearance, accent, geographic origin, personal habits, etc. It may be a little irritating at first, but you'll get used to it. You may even learn to like it.

One more thing: You will be called by your last name exclusively. No one will use your first name. In fact, you may not even know what many of your shipmates' first names are. It's strange and depersonalizing at first, but, again, you get used to it, even to the point that it will probably be a little jarring when you get to talk to your family and they call you by your first name.

The Smurf Suit. You can tell a fresh-off-the-bus Recruit by their clothing. For at least the first week, your sole outfit will be the "Smurf suit," so called because it is predominantly blue.

When it comes time to surrender your civilian clothes, you will go into the head and change into your Smurf suit. This consists of two layers; the first layer is actually your PT uniform, which is a gold t-shirt and blue shorts. (Note that you will wear your PT shorts under every uniform, at all times, during the remainder of your stay at boot camp. They become part of you.) You'll also wear your PT tube socks and tennis shoes. On top, you'll wear blue sweat pants and a blue hooded sweatshirt. To complete the look, your "valuables sock" will be worn inside the top of your pants, with the tied end sticking out. The valuables sock is just that: a tube sock in which you will deposit things like your address book, wallet, etc. You then tie a knot in the end and stick it down your pants. That little dangling end is the classic, tell-tale mark of a brand-new Recruit. That, and the look of fear and confusion.

It will probably be a few days before you are able to get your Smurf suit washed, though you will be able to change into a fresh base layer of PT gear. This means that your sweatshirt (and, let's face it, the pants, too) may become a little smelly. There will probably also be some snot stains on the sleeves. I know it's gross, but I'm keeping it real, here. You'll likely get the sniffles within a few days of arrival, and there is no kleenex in boot camp. Couple that with the fact that you will be taught that when you sneeze, you are to sneeze into your elbow rather than your hand. Plus, if you sleep in your sweatshirt, snot and drool have the knack of ending up on your cuffs. The point is, your Smurf suit is probably going to get a little nasty. But so will everyone else's, and no one's really paying attention to what you look like at this point anyway, so don't sweat it. Just try not to get big food stains on it and make your RDCs call you out for being a pig.

At night, when you remove the Smurf suit (you'll keep the shorts and t-shirt on), you'll hang it up on a hanger on your rack. There is, of course, a very specific way to do this. You're allowed to wear the pants and/or sweatshirt to bed, but at least make sure they're hung properly whenever you're not wearing them, including when you're taking a shower.

Also, be prepared for lots of blue fuzz in everything until your Smurf suit has been laundered a couple of times. The insides of the pants and sweatshirt shed lint like crazy, to the point that the resulting dust bunnies are known as "Smurf poop." Someone will have to sweep up the Smurf poop every day, possibly more than once.

A Word on Nickel Allergies

Starting the first night, you will be wearing a chain around your neck at all times. At first, this will just hold your locker key, a Sharpie and a pen, but later you'll attach your dog tags to it.

This chain is made of nickel. Some people are allergic to nickel. Right now, you probably have no idea if you are one of those people or not. If you are allergic, your neck and chest will break out in itchy bumps where the chain comes in contact with your skin.

This is common enough that Great Lakes makes available a thing called a "chain chit." This is basically a doctor's note saying that you don't need to wear your chain around your neck and can carry it in your pocket instead, or that you can wear the chain outside your undershirt so it's not touching your chest. If you are breaking out in a rash, let your RDCs know and they'll tell you what to do.

Haircuts. You will receive a haircut within a few hours of arriving at boot camp. You will look like a crazy person. (Ladies, you'll find more information on this topic just for you in the Appendix.) No matter your gender, I can virtually guarantee that this will be the worst haircut you will ever receive in your life (with the possible exception of your second boot camp haircut; there will be a second one, and possibly more, depending on how fast your hair grows).

As if looking freakish weren't bad enough, you actually have to pay for the privilege. You will hand your "stylist" your Recruit card and they will debit it for ten bucks. Awesome.

Take comfort in the fact that everyone else looks just as ridiculous as you do. Boot camp has a way of making you humble.

P-Days. The first week, or maybe even two weeks, of your time at Great Lakes is known as "P-days." The P stands for processing. This is when you will be receiving medical screenings, getting most of your uniforms and other gear, and generally just getting acquainted with life in boot camp. You will not be doing PT during P-days until everyone has passed their medical check (more on what happens after medical screening later).

In a lot of ways, your P-days will probably actually be the hardest of boot camp. They're not physically demanding, but they are stressful. These are the days when everything is new and not much makes sense. There will be a lot of information coming at you all the time, a lot of details to remember, and a lot of orders to follow. Don't be surprised if you feel pretty intimidated and maybe a little overwhelmed during these days; it happens to everyone, to some extent. This is also the time when you will be missing home because everything at Great Lakes is so foreign. You'll be in a new bed, surrounded by strangers and attempting to acclimate to a routine and an environment unlike anything you've experienced before. You may even come down with a nasty cold.

But don't let P-days get you down; it will pass, and within a few days you'll be feeling a lot better. Trust me on this. If you can make it through the first week (and you can), the rest will be pretty easy. Remember my advice about attitude, and keep this in mind: the Navy graduates hundreds of people from Great Lakes every week. What do those people have that you don't? They're not special, they're just you two months from now. Stick with it.

Different Types of Division. There are three types of division in boot camp. "Regular" divisions — or "rifle" divisions — make up the majority of divisions into which Recruits are placed. There are also so-called "900" divisions, which provide the bands, flag teams, drill teams and choirs that perform at graduation ceremonies. Then there are "800" divisions, which are for the small number of Recruits that are aiming for inclusion in elite, physically intense Navy programs like EOD, diving and rescue swimming.

There is some fuss made about the supposed elite status of 900 divisions, but don't believe the hype. As a member of one myself, I can tell you that the only difference between being in a 900 division and being in a rifle division is that 900 divisions spend a lot more time, including about four hours every Saturday, practicing drill. There is no special treatment and no privileges beyond getting to perform at graduations.

There are three kinds of 900 division: Triple Threat provides a drill team, a choir and a small band; State Flags is responsible for putting on the flag display at graduation; and Drill divisions provide rifle drillers and ceremonial guards.

A petty officer involved with the management of graduation ceremonies will come around and ask you questions to determine whether or not to place you in a 900 division. It is generally preferred that members of 900 divisions have some musical, drill or marching experience, but this is by no means a hard and fast rule. It's actually fairly arbitrary, depending on how many people they have and how many they still need. I know a fellow Sailor who has a civilian job as an instructor for a top high school marching band. He was not placed in a 900 division. On the other hand, I was. Here's how my interview for inclusion went:

Petty Officer: "Do you have any experience with marching?"

Me: "No, Petty Officer."

Petty Officer: "Do you have any experience with ROTC?"

Me: "No, Petty Officer."

Petty Officer: "Do you have any leadership experience?"

Me: "No, Petty Officer."

Petty Officer: "Can you play an instrument?'

Me: "No, Petty Officer."

Petty Officer: "Can you stand up for extended periods?"

Me: "Yes, Petty Officer."

Petty Officer: "Can you run a mile and a half?"

Me: "Yes, Petty Officer."

Petty Officer: "Can you pass the swim test?"

Me: "Yes, Petty Officer."

Petty Officer: (shrugs) "Okay, we'll try it."

And then she wrote "900" on my hand in marker and that was how I qualified as a member of a 900 division. So, no matter what your experience or lack thereof, be prepared either way.

RDCs. RDC simply stands for "Recruit Division Commander." You'll probably have three of them. They are most likely to be first-class petty officers, but may be as low as a second-class or as high as a chief.

It takes a lot to be an RDC. They have to have excellent performance records and letters of recommendation to even make it into the training program, and then they basically have to go through boot camp all over again. Not everyone who makes it into the program graduates, so you know that whoever your RDCs may be, they represent some of the best-trained, most motivated enlisted leaders the Navy has to offer. They know their stuff, and they tend to be very gung-ho about Navy life.

RDCs are pretty scary at first, but as you get to know yours, you'll probably find that underneath all that bluster and toughness, there is a layer of compassion and probably an off-color sense of humor, too. Your RDCs work even harder and get even less sleep than you do, so they are sometimes grouchy and easily irritated, but just remember that RDCs (even though they don't like to admit it) are human, too. They have likes and dislikes, which you'll quickly pick up on, they occasionally make mistakes, and deep down, they like you and want you to succeed. RDCs are there to make you into a Sailor, but they're also there to help you out and take care of you.

Red Rover. During P-days, your division will visit the medical department at the USS *Red Rover* (it's named after a Civil-War era hospital ship). This is for the purpose of doing a thorough medical and dental check so you can be qualified as Fit for Full Duty (FFD).

This is a lot like the medical screening you endured at MEPS; there's blood-drawing, a hearing test, a vision test, male and female exams, etc. There's also a dental exam where the dentist will check your teeth for cavities and other problems. They'll also see if you still have your wisdom teeth; if you do, you won't have them for long (see "A Word on Wisdom Teeth").

The exams take most of the day. If you pass all of your exams with no problem, as most people do, you'll get a stamp on your medical file saying "FFD." That means that you are cleared to do all the physical requirements of boot camp. This is also the day that you'll receive your beautiful new glasses, if you need them ("BCGs"- stands for "boot camp glasses"or the more popular "birth control glasses"). These are remarkably ugly and make you feel like you're looking through a fish bowl for a day or two, but once your eyes adjust, you'll probably find that the prescription is very accurate. Mine were actually better than my civilian glasses as far as accuracy and sharpness.

You'll return to *Red Rover* at some point for your vaccinations. There are a lot of them. A whole lot. There are shots for yellow fever, typhoid, chicken

pox, hepatitis, tetanus and a host of other things
I can't even remember. There's also one called the
"peanut butter shot," which is the only one that goes
in your butt cheek. I'm not totally sure how it got
its name—some people say it's because it's thick like
peanut butter, but I know one person who claims it
smells like peanut butter. Anyway, I do know that
it doesn't contain actual peanuts. This is the shot
that some people hear about from other divisions
and dread. It has the reputation of being extremely
painful, but it's really not quite that bad. It doesn't
feel good, but it's hardly excruciating. It does make
your butt hurt, and you can feel it spreading through
your muscle. Your leg may go a little numb or feel
heavy for a while, and you may develop a bruise, but
if you do what the corpsmen advise and use your leg
normally instead of babying it, you should be fine.
Your instinct may be to limp a little and keep weight
off that leg, but you'll end up being in much less
pain if you make yourself walk normally. It helps
the injection spread out instead of lingering in your
muscle.

There's also a flu mist that you'll have to admin-
ister yourself by sticking it up your nose. No needles
involved, just a nasal spray.

By the way, in case you're terrified of needles
and are wondering if you can opt out, the answer
is no. If you refuse any or all of the vaccinations,

you'll be dismissed from the Navy. You need these shots for your own protection and the protection of others and they are mandatory. You'll also be getting booster shots at *Red Rover* during your fifth week. There's no booster for the peanut butter shot, so that's a plus.

A Word on Wisdom Teeth

Here's something a lot of Recruits don't know until they get to boot camp; if you have wisdom teeth when you arrive, you won't have them when you leave. As unnecessary as it may seem, the Navy will remove your wisdom teeth in order to prevent problems with them down the line.

Luckily, I had had mine removed quite a few years before I went to boot camp. However, a lot of Recruits are young enough that they haven't needed to worry about wisdom teeth yet. Or, you may simply have nice, non-impacted wisdom teeth that don't really need removing. Even if this is the case, the Navy will take them. They don't care how beautiful and perfectly spaced your wisdom teeth are; they're coming out.

The procedure at boot camp is, of course, free, and this is a compelling reason to leave your wisdom teeth in for now and let the Navy dentists take them out. However, there are enough drawbacks to having it done at boot camp that I would recommend making an appointment with your dentist now and having the procedure done before you ship out.

Firstly, there is an option in the civilian world to have the surgery done under general anesthesia so you're asleep for it. The procedure at boot camp is done under local anesthesia, meaning your mouth is numb, but you're awake. Secondly, you'll be put on bed rest for a day or two afterwards and you'll have to spend your time lying on your rack, bleeding onto a towel. This is a nicer experience when you're at home. Lastly, you'll be put on a soft diet until your jaw heals. This means a lot of peanut butter and jelly sandwiches and pudding. At least if you're at home you can use it as an excuse to have ice cream and milkshakes.

Everyday Life and Routine Business

The Shape of an Average Day. Your typical day will start at 0500 or 0600. You'll make your rack, get dressed and get ready for **chow**. What happens after that will vary a bit, but there are some things that don't change:

- You will always have three meals.
- You will hygiene.
- You will get in a **height-line** before you go anywhere.
- You'll march in formation wherever you go.
- There will be a **watchbill** every day, though there are a few times when watches will be secured so that everyone can attend mandatory training (Marlinespike and firefighting, for example).

The rest of the day will be broken into things like PT, computer-based learning, lessons that take place in the compartment, classroom instruction, practicing for inspections and other pretty routine stuff. That's one of the things about boot camp that can get a little depressing or discouraging; each day, though different in its own way, is enough like every other day in its basic structure and overall predictability that it makes your time there feel longer. The things that will annoy you most are the things you have to deal with on a daily basis; marching, getting in a height line, readers, making your rack, showering in a group, reveille, standing watch and all the other little things. These are the things that can make tempers flare. The routine and the fact that you know you will have to do something that pisses you off every day can wear down your patience and your morale. My best tip for dealing with this state of mind is to keep a calendar; make a little graph of all the days between your start date and scheduled graduation date and cross one off every evening. It can be very encouraging, especially once you get about halfway through.

Hydration Policy. Within your first day or two at boot camp, you will be familiarized with the Great Lakes Hydration Policy. Yes, there really is an official policy. Yes, you will be expected to comply with it.

Basically, the policy states that you need to drink eight to ten full canteens of water every day (meaning every 24-hour period), in addition to whatever you drink at chow. If you feel like you're coming down with a cold, you should drink ten to twelve. Proper hydration is treated as sort of a magic bullet at boot camp; as my third RDC told us: "If you come to me and say, 'Petty Officer, I have a cold,' I will tell you to hydrate. If you tell me you have a headache, I will tell you to hydrate. If you fall off the dive platform at the pool and break your leg in three places, I will tell you to hydrate."

It's not as silly as it seems. There will be a lot of germs from all over the country circulating at Great Lakes, and keeping your system flushed with water will help ward them off. Plus, with all the physical activity and prolonged standing you will be doing, keeping hydrated will help you perform better and keep from passing out. You may see other benefits, too, like clearer skin, increased alertness and weight loss.

Yes, drinking that much will make you pee every ten to fifteen minutes the first couple of days, but as your body gets used to the volume of water it's taking in, you'll stop peeing quite so much. Your RDCs expect you follow the hydration policy, and they expect you to pee a lot as a consequence, so they should be pretty understanding about letting you go to the head as needed. Just don't abuse the privilege. By the way, some RDCs make their Recruits request permission to use the head, while others do not.

Pump 'n' Dumps. As you may know from a certain great work of children's literature, everybody poops. You can take a head break pretty much any time you need at boot camp, as long as you're not in the middle of something important, but there are also certain designated periods known as pump 'n' dumps. These are for the specific purpose of allow-ing you time to poop. If your RDC announces a ten or fifteen minute pump 'n' dump, you will know it's time to head for a stall and have a seat. Even if you don't need to poop, pretend like you do. You don't get much time to yourself to relax at boot camp, so take these ten precious minutes to pull the curtain on the stall and just sit for awhile. Enjoy.

Hygiene Routine. Taking a shower at home is nice: it's warm, it's refreshing, it's relaxing, it's pri-vate. Taking a shower at boot camp is a bitch.

There is really not much good to say about boot camp shower facilities, other than that they're clean. The showers are just big tiled stalls with two or three big stainless steel columns in the middle. The columns have shower heads around the top. Everyone crowds around the columns, trying to get wet enough to either lather up or rinse off. As soon as you've accomplished that, you'll be expected to move out of the way for the people next to you who aren't wet enough yet. You'll get about five to ten minutes to shower, and then you'll get dressed in the head. It's nearly impossible to get completely dry after a shower, because you'll be wearing shower shoes, and the floor will be wet, so no matter where you step, you end up with damp feet.

Anyway, before you get in the shower, you'll take all your toiletries into the bathroom in a knit bag. You'll also need to take your clean underwear, socks, and the rest of your uniform, including boots, in there. You'll also take a towel. Do not carry your towel around your neck or over your shoulder. RDCs hate that. I don't know why, but they do. I was accused by a chief of wanting to sell secrets to Osama bin Laden because I was carrying my towel over my shoulder. Something about attention to detail again. Anyway, just remember to carry your towel in your hand.

The big thing to keep in mind here is that hygiene time at boot camp is nothing like hygiene time at home. It isn't relaxing, it's far from private, and you have a very limited amount of time to accomplish anything. You might want to start practicing taking five minute showers now, just to get used to it.

Chow. The food at boot camp is actually pretty darn good. Some things are better than others, of course, but in general the food is quite tasty, and nutritious, too. Don't be afraid to try anything.

You will get three meals a day (no snacks), and you can eat as much as you want during chow time. You can't get back in line for seconds, but you can load your tray down with stuff from the salad bar, various cereals, bread, fruit, etc.

Having said that, I would urge you to be cautious and prudent about what you eat. It is possible (and common) to actually gain weight during boot camp, due to poor eating habits. You will have free access to sugary cereals, peanut butter, bread, desserts, and, on Sundays, ice cream. It is possible that your RDCs will **secure** desserts — make them off-limits — in which case you can always eat fruit instead (the fruit cups at Great Lakes are surprisingly fresh and high-quality). Even if they don't, I recommend really practicing restraint with the sweet stuff, and the peanut butter, too. Gaining weight can hurt your ability to pass your PFAs and fit in your uniforms, and there are weight restrictions in place in the Navy. If you're deemed too chunky, you'll have to lose weight or you could be separated from the service. Use boot camp as an opportunity to start getting into the best shape of your life. Try to eat a lot of salad, choose fruit instead of cookies, stay away from the peanut butter and eat what's on offer in the hot food line. It's not your mama's home cooking, but it's not bad, and you can eat whatever you want after you graduate. If you want to reward yourself, I recommend you wait until you pass your final PFA and then celebrate with some ice cream or a piece of pie. On the other hand, don't starve yourself out of concern for weight gain or out of pickiness. It takes a physical toll. A girl in my division was separated because she didn't eat properly and ended up passing out in the head and knocking herself unconscious.

The way the galley works is as follows: you'll line up in single file and wait your turn. While you're waiting, you'll be expected to be reading your Trainee Guide. As you approach the hot food line, there are several dispensers of hand sanitizer, which you will be expected to use. By the way, there is no talking in the galley. You are to eat in silence: if you need something passed to you, point to it.

There will always be two main dishes available in the hot food line, and you may pick one. If neither option is to your liking that day, you can skip ahead to the salad bar and/or the cereal. There are always condiments and peanut butter on the tables. Tea bags are available at breakfast, and coffee, milk and hot chocolate are always on offer. Near the end of the meal, a civilian will come out with a cart of dessert options and wheel it down the aisles. There will always be a fruit offering and something else a little less healthy, like cookies or pudding. When the meal is over, you'll put your tray and silverware in a little window to the scullery (dish-washing area) and head out.

A Word on Being Your Own Barista

I would now like to share with you my recipe for the Recruit Mocha. This is a tasty drink you can enjoy at breakfast or lunch that will give you a little extra pep for the next **evolution**.

Grab yourself a mug and head to the hot drinks section. Fill the mug a little less than half full with hot chocolate, then add the same amount of coffee, leaving a little room for milk. Add the milk of your choice (I recommend whole). Stir and enjoy.

Readers. You will spend a good deal of time standing at attention with the rest of your division, reciting things like your chain of command, the General Orders of a Sentry, the Sailor's Creed and other things you'll need to know for your inspections. This time is known as "readers."

It's self-explanatory and doesn't really merit a detailed discussion, but just know that you may be called upon to do it several times a day, you are expected to yell, and you must begin and end each phrase with "Petty Officer" (or "Chief" or "Sir" or "Ma'am," depending on who the most senior person present in the compartment is at the time). Bottom line: readers is extremely annoying, but it will also help you come inspection time.

The Trainee Guide. The Trainee Guide is a soft-cover book that you will literally carry with you wherever you go. It's a reference guide to pretty much all the information you will need for tests. There are sections on rank recognition, Naval history, uniform regulations, the Uniform Code of Military Justice (UCMJ), ships and aircraft, first aid, and more.

Whenever you get a chance, like when you've finished your meal and are waiting for your division's turn to leave the galley, open up your guide and do some studying. All the questions on the tests are pretty much lifted from the guide, so the more you go over the relevant sections, the better off you'll be come test time.

Marching. There was a guy who got sent back into my division for punching the guy behind him in the stomach for repeatedly stepping on his heels while marching. You may very well hear stories like this, or even witness one yourself, because nothing in boot camp makes tempers flare quite as quickly or as hotly as marching.

If you have never marched in formation before (and most of us haven't), be prepared for some fairly rough times. Not only are you expected to learn quickly, you're expected to perfect some fairly advanced marching moves for your drill inspection.

Basic marching involves just staying in step with the people around you and listening to the commands of your RPOC. It doesn't sound that complicated, but wait until you try it. You may be pretty good at it on your own, but once you're in a group of about ninety other people, things get interesting. People get out of step, heels get stepped on, feet get kicked, people trip; it can be very frustrating. There are people who never get the hang of it, but everyone makes mistakes on occasion. You'll have your heels stepped on, but you'll also step on someone else's heels at some point, so try to have patience and understanding. (That's easy to say, but it's a real challenge when the person behind you or in front of you can't get in step, or the person to your left is going too fast and you're trying to keep up). There's a pretty steep learning curve to marching, but just try your best, don't zone out and don't be afraid to ask your shipmates or an RDC for help. Better you should get help than make the people around you pissed off whenever you're going somewhere.

You'll also have to pivot around corners, even when you're on your own just walking down the P-way. It seems unnatural at first, but eventually you'll get so used to it, you may find yourself pivoting around the mall on liberty weekend. (That's one of the ways you can spot fellow freshly-graduated recruits when you're in public — they'll be in uniform, and they'll be pivoting around corners).

Keep in mind, once you graduate boot camp, you won't be marching much any more. You may have to march to and from class in A-school, but beyond that, there's not really much call for marching in the Navy. That's what the Army is for.

Folding and Stowing. Much of your life at boot camp will be spent very carefully and precisely folding things and then very carefully and precisely putting them away. There are highly, one might even say obsessively, detailed instructions on how to fold and stow just about every piece of gear you will receive, from your camos to your socks and skivvies.

The level of conformity and precision involved in folding and stowing your uniform items will seem like an absolutely ridiculous waste of time, and in the normal world you'd be right for thinking so. But boot camp is not a normal place, and you will come to realize that the reason for all this obsessive-compulsive behavior is to teach you obedience to orders and attention to detail. Pretty much everything at boot camp is designed to teach you these two things, because they're so important to good order and safety out in the fleet. Try to keep that in mind when you're folding your skivvies into a crisp little origami shape.

Your RDCs will take you through all the steps to folding and stowing each of your uniform items the first time. They'll probably give you a little copy of the instructions to stick in your notebook for future reference. After that, you'll be on your own to get it right, and yes, you'd better get it right. There is an official bunk and locker inspection, but both before and after that, your rack and locker may be inspected by your RDCs or by FQA (more on them later) at any time, without announcement. Take the time to get it right, and I recommend that you set aside a little time on Sundays to refold things and make sure they are stowed correctly. If you have a question about how to properly fold or stow something, it's okay to ask an RDC; they want you to get it right. Failed inspections reflect poorly on them.

Uniforms. There are many uniforms in the Navy, but you will really only wear one at boot camp. Once you are out of P-days, you will shed the Smurf suit and wear the Navy Working Uniform (NWUs) on a daily basis.

The NWUs are the Navy's camouflage pattern. The Navy only recently adopted this uniform; before, the everyday working uniform was blue dungarees. To bring the Navy in line with the other services, we now wear a blue-and-grey camo pattern, instead. You probably won't mind wearing this uniform as daily wear, as it is pretty comfortable. In addition to the **blouse** and trousers, it consists of a blue undershirt and a steel-toed combat boots. You'll get a little bag of little bungee-cord-like things called blousing straps. These are for your NWU trousers. Though it looks as though the trousers are worn tucked into the boots, they aren't. They are "bloused up" by putting these little blousing straps around the boots and then tucking the bottom of the pant leg up into them.

There is also a matching **cover** that goes with this uniform, but you won't be wearing that until after Battle Stations. Until then, you'll be wearing a baseball-style black cap with the word RECRUIT emblazoned on it in gold. You'll also get two pairs of coveralls. You'll only wear these a couple of times, during the last weeks of boot camp. You'll wear them for firefighting and to Battle Stations. It's kind of a bummer that you don't get to wear them more often, as they are by far the Navy's most comfortable uniform. They're kind of like footie pajamas, without the footie part.

Uniform issue happens next door to the in-processing building. The day you're set to get your uniforms, you'll put your seabag on your back and march over there. The seabag will be pretty full on the way back.

On initial uniform issue day, you'll receive four sets of NWUs, some blue t-shirts, boot socks, covers and combat boots (see "A Word on Boots" below). I was there in winter, so my initial issue also included a mock turtleneck to wear under the blouse and a parka and parka liner. I'm not sure if these are always included or if it depends on the time of year, so you may have to purchase these on your own later.

At some point, you'll go back to Uniform Issue for your service uniforms and dress uniforms. The service uniform (also known as "peanut butters" or "black and tans") are black trousers and a tan short-sleeved blouse with a white t-shirt underneath. It's worn with a black garrison cap and black dress shoes. There are two dress uniforms, summer white and winter blue. These are the classic "sailor suits." You'll wear a dress uniform at graduation.

Uniform Issue is run by civilians, some of whom are patient and nice, and others of whom are definitely not.

A Word on Boots

Your boots will need to broken in. This will take probably three or four days. This process can be very hard on your feet; quite a few Recruits end up with terrible blisters and/or shin splints, and need a sneaker chit that allows them to wear their PT shoes instead of the boots for a few days.

However, the pain and inconvenience of blisters can be avoided, at least to a significant extent. The trick is to lace up your boots as tight as they will go without cutting off your circulation. When you put the boots on, go up the laces like a ladder, tightening each pair as you go. Get the two sides of the boots as close together over the tongue as you can. They should be almost or actually touching.

This may seem counterintuitive, but the closer your boots fit to your feet, the less rubbing you'll experience and the fewer blisters you'll get. Plus, it helps the leather and insole conform to the shape of your foot for a more comfortable fit and better shock absorption.

You might also experience some shin splints or cramps in your calves at first due to the heaviness of the boots. They are steel-toed and therefore probably heavier than any shoe you are used to wearing. There's not much you can do about this, but your legs will become stronger and you'll get used to the extra weight until you don't notice it anymore. If your shin splints are really bad, go to medical. Some people try to work through shin splints and end up with hairline fractures in their shins. You can get an appropriate chit to avoid this fate.

IT. There is no way around it; you will get IT'd in boot camp. It's part of what makes boot camp what it is.

IT stands for "intensive training," but it's more commonly known as "a beating." Watch any movie involving basic training (like "Platoon" or "Jarhead") and you'll see it happen; the endless push-ups, the four-count jumping jacks, the holding of uncomfortable positions, the yelling and threats. That's IT, and it's coming your way.

Okay, I don't mean to scare you. As far as I know, no one has ever died or suffered permanent damage from getting IT'd. Some people — the ones who are already in fantastic shape — actually seem to find it somewhat amusing. I'm not one of those people, but I have undergone some pretty intense beatings and survived. It sucks more than anything while it's happening, but once it's over, you can look back on it and almost smile. There are some pretty funny stories that come out of IT sessions.

The best advice I can give you about IT is just to make a sincere effort not to quit. If you can't take anymore, you can't, but until you get to that point, try. You're not supposed to be able to withstand a two-hour IT session or to keep up with the pace of the counting. That's the point; you're not really expected to actually be able to do it, you're supposed to show enough fortitude and commitment to take your punishment. Your RDCs will be watching you, and they will be taking less note of your physical strength than your mental strength. Remember what I said about boot camp being a mental game? IT is a perfect example.

IT can be meted out to individuals for infractions, or it can be assigned to entire divisions (or anywhere in between). It may range from just enough push-ups to make you cranky to all-out, two-hour, closed-door festivals of sadism that induce puking and crying. It just depends on how badly you screwed up and what kind of mood your RDCs are in.

While you're in the midst of a beating, just try to remind yourself that, as bad as it may seem, this is actually one of the mildest forms of punishment on the spectrum. IT is for run-of-the-mill, everyday sorts of infractions like having an attitude, making a mistake while on watch, or calling a chief a petty officer. More serious infractions, like fighting, harassment, stealing or being totally out of line are dealt with much more harshly, like with a **Captain's Mast**, getting **ASMO'd** or being separated from the Navy. If you're getting IT'd, it's for a problem you can fix. Take the punishment (even if you think it's unfair), learn a lesson and move on. Everyone gets IT'd, at least as part of a division, because everyone makes mistakes. Don't take it personally.

By the way, as soon as everyone gets their "Fit for Full Duty" stamp from *Red Rover*, your division will get IT'd. It is going to happen. Your RDCs just need that stamp of approval in order to start doling out the corporal punishment, so be prepared when you see that little stamp go on your file. Your RDCs will IT you that day for two reasons: 1) Because they can, and 2) to see who has the mental toughness to take it in stride. That first IT session will say a lot about you.

PT. You will probably have PT (physical training) about three times a week. Mostly this takes place in Freedom Hall, the giant multi-story gym. You'll start with warm-ups, like various stretches, some jumping jacks, grapevines, etc. Then generally you'll run around the track for awhile or maybe do some sprints. Sometimes, instead of going to the gym and running, you'll stay in the compartment and do stretching and strengthening exercises; arm circles, push-ups, sit-ups, that sort of thing.

On Saturdays, you'll take part in a thing called BASES (Balance, Agility, Strength, Explosiveness, Stamina). This is a series of stations that you rotate through. You won't do every station any given week; which ones you do depends on where you start. You'll do this along with another division, and your team will consist of members of your own division and the other division.

The stations include hauling a stretcher with a dummy on it; weight machines; sprints; passing medicine balls down a line; jumping rope; and other fun things.

The main thing with PT, no matter what it is, is to do your best and try to have fun. Your RDCs will probably do what they can to make PT as positive as possible by singing cadence and encouraging you and maybe even letting you sing songs. Again, remember the importance of mindset; you'll be much happier in general if you try to enjoy PT than if you go in with a defeatist or negative attitude.

Classroom Instruction. I'm using this term to encompass two types of instruction; computer-based training (or CBT) and lectures.

You will do a good deal of computer-based learning at boot camp. There are lessons on all kinds of things, from Naval history to how to recognize ships and aircraft to how to field-strip a pistol. Some of it's fairly interesting, much of it is not. You can do this training more or less at your own pace, as long as you complete the lessons. In other words, if you don't make it all the way through a lesson the first time, you can complete it the next time you go to the computer lab, as well as getting started on the next lesson.

There are also good old-fashioned lectures. These will be on things like uniform regulations, sexual harassment policy, drugs and alcohol and financial issues. The best you can hope for is an instructor with a sense of humor.

Mail. Mail is a pretty big deal at Great Lakes. It's really the only reliable means of communication you'll have with the outside world. You are only guaranteed two phone calls (the thirty-second one when you first arrive and the one near the end telling your family you're ready to graduate), so the old-fashioned art of letter-writing suddenly becomes very important.

You'll have the opportunity to write letters on Sundays (if you haven't done something to really piss off your RDCs) and possibly one other day a week. Remember to put all the addresses you think you'll need in a little address book before you go. Your mailing address will be posted in your compartment.

You won't receive any mail from home until you have written home yourself, and afterwards, you'll probably find that your letters and those of your loved ones tend to overlap. The mail at Great Lakes is a little slow, but this is because there are so many Recruits to keep track of. Once your mail starts coming, it should be pretty regular.

Of course, there are rules and regulations governing mail. This won't really affect what you send out, as you won't have access to things you shouldn't

be sending out, but it does affect what you can receive. Tell your family not to send you any packages.
Pretty much anything you get from outside other
than actual letters or greeting cards is considered
contraband. This means no makeup, no toiletries, no
socks or underwear, no playing cards, no books, and
definitely no food. While I was at boot camp, someone's grandma sent them six tamales for Christmas.
That person's entire division had to do ten push-ups
per tamale, and then the RDCs ate the tamales.

Also, none of those cards that sing or fart or
whatever when you open them. Plus, you'll probably have to open anything larger or thicker than a
regular letter or card in front of your RDCs. So make
sure your family and friends understand that even
though they may be tempted to send you things they
think will brighten your day or improve your quality of life, you will get in trouble for having those
things. Tell them just to stick to regular old letters or
greeting cards. They can bring you food and books
on liberty weekend for you to enjoy at your hotel.

There is another e-book on boot camp out there
(written by former RDCs, no less) that claims that
you will be able to write letters to friends or love
interests that are also attending boot camp. THIS IS
FALSE. If you are married and your spouse is attending boot camp at the same time as you, there may
possibly be an exception made, but probably not.

Sundays. Sundays offer a bit of a break from the routine of the other days of the week. On Sundays (provided you haven't pissed off your RDCs) you will have about half a day off. I use the term "day off" sort of loosely; there are still things you will be expected to accomplish, like shining your shoes, making sure your rack is clean and other little housekeeping things like that. And of course, you will still have to make your rack and look squared away in your uniform.

If you choose to attend a religious service (see below), you may have to get up before reveille to get ready, depending on what time your service starts. I attended Catholic Mass on Sunday mornings, which required me to get up at about 0530, get dressed, have early chow and then come back to the compartment and sign out. You may not have to get up that early, but your service may still require that you eat early or late, and of course, you'll have to sign out and get an **inter-station pass** filled out.

Other than that, Sunday mornings will probably include boot-and-shoe shining, rack cleaning and maybe some ironing. You'll probably be allowed to hygiene at a time of your choosing (as long as you're done and dressed by a specified time), and you can spend the rest of the time writing letters. Since you can hygiene on your own and take more time than usual, this is the best time for ladies to shave.

You just won't get much opportunity at other times (see the "For Females" chapter). This is also a good time to clip your nails.

Now, remember, I said you get half a day off. Starting at 1300, you will be required to have an hour of "field day." This is the Naval term for cleaning the hell out of an area, top to bottom. So, you'll be **swabbing** the floor, making sure racks are made correctly and tightly, dusting, scrubbing the heads and showers, shining the **scuttlebutt**, cleaning the windows of the shark tank, chasing dust bunnies, sanitizing the canteens with bleachy water, and generally making sure your compartment and everything in it is shiny and clean. This will last an hour, and then you'll get on with other scheduled business.

Sleeping Arrangements and Racks. Sleep is a precious commodity at boot camp. You'll never really feel like you've had enough of it. This is due to several factors: You'll be doing a lot during the day and will get tired out; you'll be sleeping in a room full of other people who may snore or grind their teeth or whatever; you'll have to get up in the middle of the night almost every night to iron or stand watch or both; and there are always lights on in the compartment.

Your RDCs and official Navy policy want you to believe that you'll get eight hours of sleep every night. This is simply not true. It is true that your bedtime will be eight hours before your wake-up time, but this does not mean that you will spend all that time sleeping. There are things to do even at night. You may have to stand watch during the night. You will be expected to get up and spend half an hour every night ironing your shirts and underwear (yes, I am totally serious — you will be ironing your underwear). There may be a time when, for whatever reason, you may miss your division's scheduled hygiene time (you may be standing watch, for example, or perhaps visiting medical or any number of other things). You will then have to hygiene immediately after taps.

Basically, what I'm trying to say is, once you are out of P-days, you will almost never get a full eight hours of sleep. You will get at most seven and a half, and often more like six. There were a couple of times when, between standing watch and ironing, I got three hours of sleep. Lack of sleep is a constant problem at boot camp. This is a big reason why you sit on the floor and aren't allowed to lean on things; if you're even minimally comfortable, you will fall into a coma. Sleepiness particularly becomes a problem when you're doing CBTs or attending a classroom lecture. Don't be embarrassed to just admit you're falling asleep and stand up. If you fall asleep in class, you will get in trouble and the people sitting next to you will get in trouble for not keeping you awake. Just stand up; it's what you're supposed to do.

You will never feel well-rested. You'll fall asleep shining your shoes, writing letters, sitting on the toilet, or any time you stop moving for a few minutes. In fact, it's not uncommon for people to fall asleep while standing at attention or even while marching. Everyone deals with it, but you don't have to get in trouble for it; be aware of when you're nodding off and do something about it. Don't put the responsibility of keeping you awake on your shipmates.

The position of your rack in the room will have quite a bit to do with how well you sleep. If your RDCs are nice enough to let you choose your bunk, try not to get a rack next to the head, as the lights stay on in there all night and there are people using the toilets and sinks at all hours. Likewise, try to avoid the racks nearest the compartment door, as there tends to be traffic in and out even during the night, and the deck log station is right there, too. The watch standers need to talk to each other and perform weapon turnovers. If you're a heavy sleeper, of course, you might be perfectly comfortable wherever your rack is.

The racks come in pairs; they're basically bunk beds. The main drawbacks of a top bunk are that you have to climb up and down when you need to get in or out of your rack, and there are no ladders. Also, if your bunk is right under one of the red **running lights** that are turned on at taps, you'll have no shelter from it. The main disadvantages of a bottom rack are that if you forget where you are and sit up suddenly, you'll bang your head, and that your bunkmate will have to step on your bed in order to get up and down. I slept in a top rack the first night but was able to move a bottom rack after that. Personally, I much preferred the bottom.

Your rack has two components; the bed itself and the locker. The bed lifts up like a lid and there's a compartment underneath where all your gear will be stored. This locker is not, in fact, lockable. An RDC or inspector can open it up at any time and have a look around. However, there is a small personal drawer, called an A/B drawer (I have no idea why), in which you'll keep your toiletries and personal items you don't want messed with, like your valuables sock. Hint: It's also a great place to temporarily store any dirty laundry that didn't get collected. You don't want unwashed socks or skivvies in your locker, in case of inspection.

You'll be grateful to get into your rack every night because, like I said, you'll always be tired. You might not notice that the mattresses are made out some kind of hard foam material covered in plastic or that your wool blanket is kind of scratchy.

Speaking of blankets; for probably the first week or so, you'll have to strip your rack of sheets, blanket and pillow case every morning, so you can practice making your rack properly and quickly. After this, however, you probably won't have to take the sheets off every morning, so you can take a little shortcut to making your rack. This advice might sound a little weird, but believe me, it works and it's awesome: Don't sleep under your sheets. Once you've got your sheets properly configured, leave them just the way they are. Then, you'll only have to tweak them and smooth them out in the morning to get them looking right. Sheets are washed once a week, so you can sleep under your sheets the night before that, because you'll just strip them off and trade them in in the morning. So, if you use the top-of-sheet sleeping method, you'll only have to completely fix your rack once a week. You can just use your blanket at night and fold it up in the morning, which takes maybe a minute or two. Try it. You'll like it.

You won't be allowed to sit or lay on your rack during the day. You can sit on the floor at the end of your rack if you need to shine your shoes or study.

Jobs. There are a host of jobs you can do at boot camp, if you are so inclined. I would never go so far as to say that you shouldn't volunteer for anything at boot camp, but if you want a job, it would be unfair of me not to let you understand what you'll be getting yourself into.

Any divisional job, no matter how small it seems, comes with a lot of responsibility and extra expectations. If you're the recruit chief petty officer, you'll be in overall charge of the entire division, second to the RDCs. Talk about pressure. Yeomen, likewise, have a ton of responsibility and are often in trouble. Same with the port and starboard watches. Even the laundry and mail POs tend to be under quite a bit of pressure. So, by all means, volunteer for a job if you want one, but be very mindful of the extra time and accountability that will be demanded of you.

I mentioned a few positions just now, and you probably had no idea what I was talking about. So, just what are the divisional jobs available? Here's the rundown:

- Recruit Chief Petty Officer (RPOC): Pronounced "arpock." This is the toughest and most demanding job in the division. You must have excellent leadership skills and the ability to command respect. You must also be very good at marching, since you will lead the division when they march and during drill inspection. If there are any disciplinary or attitude problems in the division, or if the division is ever late for an appointment, it's ultimately your fault as far as the RDCs are concerned.

• Assistant Recruit Chief Petty Officer (AROC): Pronounced "a-rock." In addition to being the second-in-command to the RPOC, the AROC will call cadence when the division marches, so if you want this job, you should be able to sing pretty well, and loudly. This is another high-responsibility, high-expectation position.

• Yeomen — Pronounced "yo-men." There are several yeomen (not "yeomans") in the division. There will be a lead yeoman, a medical yeoman, a dental yeoman and maybe a couple more yeomen, at the RDCs' discretion. Yeomen are responsible for all divisional paperwork and record-keeping, and take muster (i.e. call the roll) at different points during the day. Yeomen, especially the lead yeoman, tend to be constantly busy. There are innumerable forms to fill out and records to check on a daily basis. The lead yeoman will also carry a pouch wherever he or she goes, containing things like muster rolls, a copy of the watchbill, and tampons and pads for the ladies. Yeomen get their pouches inspected a lot.

• Port and Starboard Watches: One for each compartment. For example, my division's port watch was in the male compartment and the starboard watch was in the female compartment. Which one you are depends on the position of your compartment; whether it's on the port side or starboard side of the "ship." The two watches are responsible for making the watchbills every day and for making sure the deck log is properly filled out and mistake-free. This can also be a stressful job, as a lot of importance is placed on proper watchstanding and the correct use of the deck log (see the "Watchstanding"section). You'll need very good **Recruit handwriting** and grammar and spelling skills. You'll also lead the port and starboard sections, respectively, when the division is in formation, so it helps to be good at marching.

• Masters-at-Arms: There are two of these, again, one for each compartment. You're basically the divisional police, responsible for maintaining good order and discipline. You'll need to be confident and authoritative, without being a hothead or a tyrant.

• Guidon: Pronounced like "guide on." This person is responsible for carrying the divisional flag (also called the guidon) while marching, and for the proper care and maintenance of any other flags the division earns. The ideal guidon is on the short side, has good marching skills and has maybe a touch of OCD. The more perfectionistic you are as a guidon, in your own performance and in the care of the flags, the better you'll be at your job.

• Other Recruit Petty Officers: There are several other Recruit Petty Officer (or "PO") positions available. They are : Mail PO; Religious PO, who lets everyone know about services and makes a list of who wants to attend; Athletic PO, who helps lead the division in exercises and keeps track of PT-related records; Educational PO, who guides study sessions and provides tutoring for tests; and two Laundry POs. These are the ones your division will definitely have, and there may be other PO positions available, or assistants to the POs, at your RDCs' discretion.

• Flags: When your division achieves certain standards, you will be awarded a flag for that accomplishment. For example, if everyone in your division passes all the tests, you'll get the Academic flag. If you pass all your PFAs you'll get the Athletic flag, etc, etc. There are several flags you can earn, and each time you earn a flag, someone will need to carry that flag. The people who carry these other flags are simply called flags. Flags will need to be good marchers and will spend many hours practicing their moves for the drill inspection.

- Section Leaders — Each row of racks will have a leader. These section leaders are chosen for their neatness and skill at folding and stowing. They are responsible for making sure the racks and lockers in their section are up to standards. If you have a question about how to fold or stow something, or about how to properly make your rack, your section leader is the go-to person.
- Other jobs around the compartment — There will be a variety of other, non-official jobs as well. For example, there will be the Nasty Nine (or perhaps the Dirty Dozen) in each compartment, responsible for keeping the head clean. There will also probably be someone in charge of sweeping for dust bunnies every morning, or of making sure racks are properly made. If there's a job that needs doing on a daily basis, chances are someone or a team of people will be put in charge of it.
- Ship's Staff — There is one more kind of job, for which you can be nominated, instead of volunteering. If your RDCs see that you have particularly good military bearing and good discipline, they may choose you for Ship's Staff. This is beyond the division and outside the compartment. Each ship has its own staff, and they are responsible for manning the **quarterdeck** (the main lobby), standing ship-wide

roving watches, and performing cleaning and maintenance tasks, like swabbing or buffing, as needed. There is a watch on the quarterdeck at all times, and there are rovers at night, so being on Ship's Staff may require you to take on extra watches, in addition to your regular compartment watches.

No matter what your job is, the main traits you'll need are responsibility, leadership, level-headedness and good old-fashioned common sense. Humility doesn't hurt, either. And even if you don't have a regular job, make sure you help out the people who do. Help sweep the floor every once in a while, keep the head clean, and have good discipline. Don't make anyone carry you.

Sick Call. Sick call happens twice a day, once in the morning and once in the evening. This is the time when, if you're not feeling well, you can visit a medic. Each ship has its own sick call location. You can sign yourself out to sick call at your own discretion; your RDCs can't keep you from going. However, make sure you really are feeling bad before you go. Don't go just because you want some time out. That spells trouble.

Now, I can't tell you exactly what happens at sick call, since I personally never went. I do know that the Navy's answer to just about every illness or minor injury is a couple of Motrin and maybe an ice pack. I would recommend that you avoid sick call unless you have an infection, like pink eye, or you suspect you may have an injury that could get worse with exertion, like a pulled or torn muscle. Otherwise, it's just kind of a waste of time. If you have a cold, you can get a "cold pack," which is some decongestants and some tissue, or you can get a handful of lozenges for a sore throat, but that's about it.

On the subject of pink eye, this nasty infection has a bad habit of running rampant at RTC. First of all, everyone lives in very close quarters, so it's easy for the bacteria to jump from person to person. Secondly, you'll spend a lot of time sitting on the floor. People walk around with dirty boots on that floor, then you sit down and put your hand on the floor, and then you touch your face and BANG!—pink eye. Wash and sanitize your hands a lot and try to remind yourself not to touch your face. If you do end up with an itchy, oozy eyeball, go to sick call and get some antibiotics before it gets worse.

Going to the NEX. At some point, probably once you're out of P-days, your RDCs will take you on a trip to the NEX, the Navy Exchange. This is basically a big convenience store. Think Walgreen's, but without the medicine.

You'll be able to buy things like body wash, shampoo, deodorant, maybe some lotion, things like that. Keep in mind that exactly what things you can buy is up to your RDCs; if they want everyone to have the same kind of body wash, that's what you're stuck with. They should make it clear as to what you can get before you go. If you're unsure on something, ask one of your RDCs before you purchase. Also, there may be a few items they require you to buy, so the division can share them. This will be stuff like pads for the females, and athlete's foot spray.

As you get low on supplies, you'll be allowed to make another trip as a division. If you run completely out of something and the division isn't ready to make a NEX run yet, you may be able to arrange an individual or small group visit with your RDCs' approval.

The NEX is also where the phone bank is. You'll be able to make a phone call after Battle Stations to tell your family you're ready to graduate. Other than that, how many phone calls your division gets is totally up to your RDCs. If your division does something particularly worthy, you may be rewarded with a phone call. On the other hand, scheduled phone calls can also be taken away or shortened if your division screws up.

Pictures. You'll have your picture taken twice at boot camp. One will be an individual picture and the other will be a group photo. Both photos will be taken in your dress uniform.

Don't expect to look particularly good in either picture. Females may be allowed to wear a modicum of makeup, and you'll be allowed to take off your hideous glasses, but it's pretty much impossible to look your best at boot camp. Take heart, though; the individual picture will be digitally enhanced, meaning that they'll take out any flyways and big zits. Plus, the dress uniforms help a lot toward making anyone look good.

You'll be able to order a package of photos. You'll receive the package shortly before your scheduled graduation date and then you can send them home with your loved ones during liberty weekend.

⚓

Watchstanding

Standing watch is a constant feature of every-day life at boot camp, and I think that it's important enough to merit its own section, instead of just being included in the "Routine Business" section. There are a lot of duties and responsibilities involved, so it's best to deal with them on their own.

On a ship, there are always people standing watch in the different sections. Watchstanders ensure that everything is squared away, safe and secure. They watch for fires and guard against intruders, and make sure that everyone is where they're supposed to be and doing what they're supposed to be doing. Standing watch at boot camp prepares you for this important duty (pretty much everyone stands watch in the fleet). You will also stand watch in A-school.

Knowing how to stand a proper watch is essential to safety and good order in the fleet, and so it is taken very seriously at boot camp. Like anything, standing watch gets easier the more you do it, but at first it can be intimidating and may even seem a little confusing. I'm going to give you a quick orientation of what a watch is and how its duties are performed.

The Very Basics of Watch. Think of a watchstander as a security guard. You will be standing watch in your compartment, and while you are on watch, you have authority over, and responsibility for, what

goes on in that compartment. You will be expected to maintain good order and discipline among
whoever is in the compartment, make sure the racks,
laundry room and head are on-spot, check for safety
issues, and know who is coming and going. You will
challenge visitors and record everything you do
and what you observe in the deck log. Sometimes, if
someone is sick, they will be put on bed rest. You will
be responsible for checking on that person periodically and making sure they're okay (and also that
they're not getting out of bed and farting around).
There are instances of Recruit watchstanders saving
the lives of bedridden shipmates who had stopped
breathing or gone unconscious.

Once your division has passed your weapon
turnover inspection, you will carry a gun on watch.
The gun will be loaded, but will have had its firing
pin removed, so you can't actually shoot anyone.

Watch goes on 24 hours a day. Unless watch is
secured because of mandatory training, there will
always be someone on watch in your compartment.
If you are berthed with another division, usually one
division takes day watches and the other takes night
watches, alternating every day.

Every day, your watch coordinator, with the
approval of your RDCs, will create a watchbill. This
is a list of everyone who has watch that day, from
0600 in the morning until 0600 the next morning.

It is your responsibility to check the watchbill every day for your name. In fact, it's a good idea to check it a couple of times throughout the day, because occasionally changes must be made.

Watches during the day, from **reveille** until **taps**, are four hours long, while night watches are two hours. If you have watch during the day, you may need to go to chow earlier or later than the rest of your division so as not to conflict with your watch time. There will be a chart in your compartment telling you what time to eat chow according to which watch you have. Again, it is your responsibility to know these things and take care of them.

You may also miss your division's scheduled hygiene time. If this is the case, you will have to hygiene immediately following taps and then clean up the shower after yourself. This is not an excuse to stay up late and hang out after taps. You will need to hygiene quickly and go to bed.

You may miss out on other things as well, like non-mandatory CBTs or PT. But rest assured, you will never miss anything essential because of watch. On days when mandatory training or testing are going on, either someone from the other division you are berthed with will take over, or watch will be secured for that period.

The Deck Log. The deck log is a very big deal. When my division started standing watch on our own, our RDCs arranged for a visit from another RDC who called himself the Deck Log King. He gave us a great orientation to the purpose of the deck log and the proper procedures for filling it out, and I'll pass as much of that information on to you as I think is relevant, without weighing you down with details you'll be familiarized with at Great Lakes.

Like I said, the log a big deal. Consider this exchange between the Deck Log King and my division:

Deck Log King: "I love my deck log like I love my own daughter. If I let you come to my house and babysit my daughter and when I came home she had a bruise from falling down the stairs, what do you think I would do to you?"

Division: "Fuck us up, Petty Officer."

Deck Log King: "That's correct, I would fuck you up. And I will fuck you up if you fuck up my deck log."

The deck log is actually a legal document, and each one is kept in the Great Lakes archives for several years. If someone wants to know where you were at any given time during your stay at boot camp, they can check the log.

So, exactly what is the purpose of the deck log? Well, it's basically a record of what happened in the compartment during each watch period. When you come on watch, you record that you took over the watch. When you go on a periodic rove of the compartment, you record what time you left and when you came back. If you find something off-spot, like laundry in the dryers, you note that. If an inspector comes in, you note it. When the division leaves, you note the time and where they went. If someone leaves the compartment after taps and before reveille, you take their name and destination.

Since the deck log is an official document, and because FQA just loves to come around and inspect deck logs for even the tiniest of errors, it is imperative that you use your best Recruit handwriting, that you spell and punctuate correctly, and that you write the correct times down. If you have a question as to whether or not something should be noted in the log, ask your watch coordinator or an RDC. Don't ever guess. If you have any questions at all about log entries, even if it's just how to spell something or where to put a comma, ask.

If you do make a small mistake, it's possible to fix it. For example, if you meant to write 1245 and accidentally put 1230, put a single straight line through the mistake (use a ruler), make the correction underneath, and initial your correction. Don't panic if you make a mistake; that tends to make it worse. Just one-line it and correct it. You should also let your watch coordinator know if you make a mistake, just so they're aware. Ultimately, they are responsible for whatever gets put down in the log, so don't let your mistakes get them in trouble.

Nothing teaches you attention to detail quite so well or thoroughly as using the deck log. If you pay attention and do well making entries, you will be an asset to your whole division, because it will help keep the inspectors off your back and out of your RDCs' hair, and your watch coordinator will be grateful, too.

Types of Watch. In boot camp, there are two types of watch. Roving watch or "rover" is constant, while sentry watch only takes place at night, from taps until reveille.

A rover's job is to make entries in the deck log, challenge visitors and make a fifteen-minute round of the entire compartment every half-hour. You'll make sure towels and blankets are folded and hung properly, shoes are aligned with wheels, the head has enough paper towels and toilet paper, and generally that the compartment is safe and as on-spot as possible. Like I mentioned, you are also responsible for order and discipline if there are recruits in the compartment.

In addition to the rover, there is a sentry at night. The sentry's job is basically to stand in one spot and watch the compartment door. When the rover goes on a round, the sentry will step up to the deck log and make any necessary entries while the rover is gone. The sentry will also challenge night-time visitors, along with the rover. Also, the sentry and rover will be responsible for waking up any Recruits who need to be up early (they'll put their names on a wake-up list).

Reporting for Watch. A watch actually begins fifteen minutes before the scheduled time. In other words, if you have the 2000 watch, you'll actually begin your watch at 1945. Plus, you'll want to be at least fifteen minutes early for your watch, so in reality you'll be reporting for watch at 1930. If you have a night watch, this means the person you'll be taking over for will probably wake you up about 45 minutes before the scheduled watch time. Don't make them ask you twice; it's rude and very frustrating for the other person. They shouldn't need to worry about whether their replacement is going to be on time. If you know you are a heavy sleeper and difficult to awaken, be responsible and let the person you'll be taking over for know that, so they can start attempting to wake you well ahead of time.

When you report for your watch, you'll go through the weapon turnover procedure, the previous watch will let you know of any issues they encountered, and you'll properly relieve that person (which simply involves saluting them and saying, "You are properly relieved.") They will sign out and you will then note in the log that you have taken over a new watch. All this is why you need to be at least fifteen minutes early.

A Word on Watchstanding Courtesies

There is nothing wrong with being more than the regulation fifteen minutes early for your watch. If you relieve your predecessor earlier than expected, chances are good that that person will reciprocate the favor one day if they get the chance. This is especially appreciated at night.

Similarly, don't be closed-minded about taking over someone's watch for them. Someone may come to you and ask to switch times, or promise to take over a future watch for you if you'll take theirs today. *Don't make any switches without the permission of your watch coordinator*, because he or she will need to get the permission of an RDC to change the watchbill, but keep in mind that doing favors for shipmates often pays off when you want a similar favor.

Let your watch coordinator know of any deck log mistakes, by you or someone else. (Don't fix other people's mistakes, just let the coordinator know so they can take care of it). While you're standing around waiting for your next rove, it's a good idea to go back in the log a few watch periods and check for any previous mistakes that weren't caught. Your watch coordinator will appreciate it — and it never hurts to be on the watch coordinator's good side.

Last but certainly not least, don't deliberately try to come off as a bad watchstander. Some people hate standing watch and decide that they will do something shitbaggy, like writing sloppily in the deck log or not fixing little things that are off-spot, because they think this will prevent them from being put on the watchbill again. Not so. You'll get yourself and probably your watch coordinator in trouble, and you may well find your name on the watchbill more often. Your RDCs will probably figure that you need more opportunity for practice.

Special Instruction and Other Requirements

The Swim Test. You can't be in the Navy if you can't swim. Makes sense, right? So, to ensure that you could in fact save yourself if your ship went down, you will have to pass a swim test before you can graduate.

I am a pretty good swimmer myself, so I wasn't particularly worried about the test, but I have to admit that it was a bit harder than I had anticipated. The pool is 50 yards long, which is a long way to go without being able to stop. And that's just the beginning; there are three parts to the test, and you must pass all three.

The morning of your test, you will assemble a "swim roll." This consists of a towel, a soapy loofa in a baggy, your shower shoes, a fresh undershirt and PT shorts, and skivvies, all packed into a **knit bag**. You'll probably wear your bathing suit under your clothes.

The first portion of swim day consists of some classroom instruction about the necessity of being able to swim. After that, you'll strip down to your bathing suit and take a quick shower to rinse it and yourself off. Then you will sit on the bleachers, dripping wet and freezing, until it's your turn.

On your turn, you will ascend the diving platform (it's about ten feet high) and cross your arms over your chest. You will step to the edge, take a deep breath, and pinch your nose shut. Make sure you pinch it tight! My grip on my nose came loose when I hit the water and I got quite a bit of water up my nose, which made me choke and made it very difficult to take a normal breath. It affected my ability to swim freestyle and I had to backstroke the whole way.

Anyway, the instructor on the platform will count down from three. When he says "Step!" you will lift your foot to step and then he will put his hand on the small of your back and push you off. Hey, at least you don't have to worry about losing your nerve and not being able to jump...

The rest of this portion is straightforward; you just swim to the other end of the pool. You can freestyle, backstroke, sidestroke or breaststroke, and you can change strokes if you get tired. It's pretty easy if you can already swim, but remember that it is a long way, and you're not allowed to stop.

Once you have passed this initial portion, there are two more to go. Next, you will put on a pair of coveralls, get in the water and use the coveralls as a flotation device by slapping air into them. It sounds a little weird, but it will make total sense once you see it done.

The last part is a test of your ability to float and tread water. You will spend five minutes alternating between treading water and floating face down. Again, pretty easy, but five minutes can seem like a long time when you're already tired from your swim.

The big thing to remember for all three parts is just to stay calm. Listen to instruction, do exactly as you're told, and relax. The more nervous you are, the more you'll tire yourself out and the more prone you will be to make a mistake. If you're scared of water (in which case joining the Navy is a slightly odd choice, but it happens), just remember that all the instructors at the pool are certified, highly trained Navy divers and swimmers. There are lots of them, and they will rescue you if something untoward occurs.

If you cannot swim, I cannot stress enough the value of taking some lessons now. If you can't find swimming lessons or facilities where you are, well, I'm not going to lie to you: you will be at a severe disadvantage come swim test day. I'm not saying this to scare you, because you can still pass the test, I just want to give you the reality. There will be instructors there who can give you some quick, basic instructions in swimming right before the test. Realistically, this probably won't be a hell of a lot of help to you, but the good news is that if you don't pass the swim test, you can continue taking it until you do pass. The bad news is, you will be required to return to the pool every day until you do. There was a guy in my division who didn't pass the swim test until the day before Battle Stations. (If you don't pass before your division runs Battle Stations, you will be held back). Having to go to the pool every day is not an ideal situation, obviously, as it requires you to miss out on other things and creates just that much more stress on you. However, it does happen, quite often, and it's not the end of the world. But if you can possibly arrange some lessons before you go to boot camp, by all means do so. It will be worth it.

Marlinespike. "Marlinespike" is just good, old-fashioned deckhand seamanship. It's all about tying knots and handling line. There are two sessions of classroom instruction involved, followed by a trip to the creatively named USS *Marlinespike*, a simulated half-ship where you will demonstrate the skills you've learned.

One classroom session will be dedicated to linehandling, which will be demonstrated to you, and to using a sound-powered telephone. It's a little confusing, frankly, and it's a lot of information to absorb, so pay close attention. Passing your test at the USS *Marlinespike* will depend on this information.

You will learn how to cast off line from a ship and from the pier, how to secure a ship to the pier with line and how to wrap line around a cleat. You will then learn the proper procedures for talking on a sound-powered telephone, using a script. Pay special attention to the safety precautions they give you (especially about stepping over lines and putting your knees down on the deck). Safety violations are the number one reason why points get deducted from your division on USS *Marlinespike* day.

I'm not going to go into detail about linehandling, because it's pretty much impossible to practice on your own. Plus, it's all in the training guide; study, pay attention and don't get flustered.

The next classroom session will focus on knot tying, nautical flags and safety. Again, this is all in your training guide. Just make sure you take time to study.

At the USS *Marlinespike*, you will break into teams and demonstrate what you've learned, as well as your ability to work as a team. This involves:

- Throwing a line from the ship to the pier
- Catching the line at the pier and securing the ship with it
- Wrapping line around cleats
- Tying a bowline knot
- Raising and lowering the ensign
- Responding to a "man overboard" alarm, and
- Communicating via sound-powered telephones

Not everyone will have to do everything, but be ready for anything because you don't know what you'll be assigned to do beforehand. And remember what I said about being mindful of safety violations.

By the way, teamwork really does count here; the instructors will be judging your unit cohesiveness and they will report to your RDCs on it. My division was smart, but we had a lot of egos and never really learned to come together as a team. Boy, did we pay for it. Let's just say our post-marlinespike experience involved more push-ups and mountain-climbers than any human can reasonably be expected to withstand. There was puke, sweat and even a few tears. You've been warned.

Damage Control and Firefighting. As your instructors will tell you, every sailor is a firefighter. Pretty much no matter what your rating is, if you are assigned to a ship once you get to the fleet, you will be placed on a hose team. Each hose team is assigned a section of the ship, and they will be the first responders should something start to leak or suddenly burst into flame in that section. There are Damage Controlmen who are dedicated to taking care of these things, but there may come a time when you or your team needs to stop a leak or get a handle on a fire before the DCs can get there. This is where your damage control and firefighting training come into play.

Damage control encompasses mechanical repairs, emergency procedures and the use of protective gear. One day of classroom instruction will be devoted to learning to "brace for shock," how to find your way around a ship using compartment numbers (good luck with that), putting a patch on a leaky pipe, and understanding material conditions settings. (Again, use the training guide early and often). You will also watch some fairly traumatizing films about great Naval disasters like the fire aboard the USS *Forrestal* and the bombing of the USS *Cole*. Drink a lot of coffee the morning of your first damage control class; it's a long day in a stuffy classroom.

Your firefighting classroom session will focus on how to don firefighting and CBRE gear. Pay close attention. There are a lot of steps, and this will be critical knowledge during Battle Stations. After learning how to put on firefighting gear, you will learn how to put on a gas mask. You will then be taken to a sealed chamber and gassed. More on that in a moment.

The hands-on portion of firefighting is a big deal in terms of giving you skills you absolutely must have in order to pass Battle Stations. (Hint, hint.) While the information is critical, don't let the instructors or your RDCs make it more intimidating than it really is. You will have to navigate through a smoky, dark chamber, use a fire extinguisher and then put out a fire as part of a hose team. All of this sounds pretty daunting, but believe me, it isn't. It's almost disappointingly easy, as long as you remember the steps and do as you're told. "Putting out the fire" does involve real water and real fire, but you know you've been successful when the instructor flips the switch and turns the flame off. It's not scary, it's not particularly hot, the flames aren't close to you, and you pretty much can't fail unless you're a total asshole or a hopeless idiot. However, keep in mind the advice I gave in the Marlinespike section about teamwork.

The Confidence Chamber. I love the smell of tear gas in the morning. And so will you after you've survived the Confidence Chamber.

Okay, I don't, and you won't either, but the Confidence Chamber is something you will not forget. Whether it kicks your ass or just makes you feel like you've been chopping onions, being sealed in a room full of lachrymatory agent is an experience you will be talking about later.

The Confidence Chamber gets its name from the fact that it is meant to give you confidence that a gas mask does, in fact, protect you from poisonous vapors. The Navy demonstrates that to you in the most immediate, hands-on way possible; you get to experience the difference between being in a gas-filled atmosphere with a mask and being in a gas-filled atmosphere without a mask.

You will be taught how to don a gas mask and ensure you have a seal (having a seal means that there's no outside air leaking in around the edges of the mask). As a division, you will then file into the gas chamber. You will stand in rows, one behind the other, and wait while one instructor prepares the tear gas and another tells you what to do. This is the time when nerves start to run high. They will probably tell you to relax and bounce up and down a bit (known as "doing popcorns") so you don't pass out.

The tear gas by now will be popping and sizzling, and they'll turn a fan on to circulate it. You will be told, "There is gas in this chamber. You have a seal. You are fine." And you are. The gas mask does work. You'll find out just how well it works in a moment.

The gassing goes by rows. On the command, "Masks up, cups up," the people in the first row will remove their masks with one hand and put their other hand under their faces, to catch the snot and spit. One by one, they will recite their name, division and social security number. When the whole row has done this, that row gets to exit the chamber. And then the next row goes, and so on. If you're in the last row, by the way, that's bad news for you. The gas will have been building up for quite some time, and it's going to be that much more powerful.

I am told that tear gas has a greater effect on males than on females, and from what I saw on my Confidence Chamber day, it seems to be true. The guys generally had a lot more snot and spit to deal with than the girls did. Anyway, after you are gassed you will go to the head and wash your hands. You must not, however, get water on your face, as it will make the burning worse. The runny nose and uncontrollable salivation stop pretty much immediately once you are out of the chamber, and the burning should stop after about five to ten minutes.

Remember that tear gas isn't quite the same for any two people; some people are barely affected, others have a really tough time. Most people fall somewhere in between. You don't know until you do it, but you will survive it.

The Firing Range. This is definitely one of the best parts of boot camp, once you get past the dry classroom instruction. I'd never fired a gun in my life before live-fire day, and I was pretty nervous, but I have to say that my experience at the firing range was a blast, no pun intended.

Day one of weapons instruction involves some classroom time and then a practice run with laser guns. This phase is known as SAM-T. The replica pistols and shotguns are meant to familiarize you with the look and feel of firing the real thing, but honestly, I found them much more difficult to use than the real guns. I think the aim is less accurate than with a real pistol. I struggled with my aim and a petty officer pulled me off the line for individual instruction, and he was not nice to me. This difficulty is why I was nervous the next day at the live-fire range. I figured I would do pretty horribly.

Day two is when the fun really starts. Like I said, I was nervous, afraid I'd screw up, but when the time came, I pulled my M9 out of the holster, flipped the safety off and locked right in. I was calm and I had a great time. I ended up earning a pistol sharpshooter ribbon (see below), of which I am still inordinately proud.

As always, listening to instruction and not jumping the gun (again, no pun intended) is of paramount importance here. Do exactly as your supervisor tells you when he tells you to do it. Remember to take your finger off the trigger and put the safety on when you're not shooting, always point the barrel of the gun straight ahead, and keep your eyes forward. These are the most common safety violations, and if you repeatedly make mistakes like these, your supervisor will more than likely pull you off the line and your day of shooting will be over.

Once you have completed your pistol course of fire, you'll have a few minutes with the M500 shotgun. This part is really easy, because you don't really have to aim a shotgun; the spread takes care of the aiming. All you need to do is keep the barrel level with the **deck** and fire away. The gun will be loaded with low-recoil rounds, so it won't kick really hard.

You'll be shown how to "combat load" the shotgun with four shells and you'll fire three times from the shoulder and once from the hip. It's a lot of fun and you'll feel like a badass when you're done.

Live-fire day is a chance to win yourself some **chest candy**. Depending on how well you shoot, you can qualify for a pistol ribbon. There are also two higher modifications to this ribbon, sharpshooter and expert. Pretty much no one gets expert, but it's something to aim for (that pun was intentional). If you qualify as a sharpshooter, you get to put a little bronze "S" on your pistol ribbon, and for experts it's a silver "E."

And ladies, take heart: it's a proven fact that females tend to score better than males at pistol shooting. This is because most females have never shot a gun before, so they actually listen to instruction, do exactly as they're told, and don't go all trigger-happy. Most guys either figure they know it all already or they get so excited they forget to aim or follow all the safety steps. Get out there and earn yourself an "S," girl!

Tests. There are three computer-based tests you must pass. If you don't pass one the first time, you will be given another shot. If you fail the second time around, you'll be set back into another division that hasn't taken that test yet and you will therefore graduate a week or two later than scheduled. So, study.

Also, if your division gets good individual scores, your division will be eligible for an academic flag.

The tests are as follows: Test 1 covers the UCMJ; first aid; ships and aircraft; rank recognition; and uniforms and grooming. Test 2 covers conduct during armed conflict; military customs and courtesies; equal opportunity policy; basic seamanship; and Naval history. Test 3 is on antiterrorism and force protection; damage control; safety and firefighting gear; the chemistry and classes of fire; and firefighting procedures. Keep in mind that each test will include a handful of questions on material from the earlier test, so Test 2 will have some questions from Test 1, and Test 3 will have questions from Tests 1 and 2.

PFAs. You will perform three PFAs. The first is to get a baseline, the second is to see how you've improved and the third is the one you must pass in order to graduate. Don't let your RDCs make it seem as though it is mandatory to pass all three. It isn't.

Obviously, it will be much less stressful for you if you do pass the first two, or at least the second one, but these do not actually count toward whether or not you graduate. It's just the third one that really, truly counts.

As I mentioned toward the beginning of the book, there are three parts to the PFA. You must do push-ups, sit-ups and a run of a mile and a half. How many you must do and how fast you must run vary according to your sex and age. Here are the minimum requirements:

Age / sex		Sit-ups	Push-ups	Run time
17–19	M	50	42	12:30
	F	50	19	15:00
20–24	M	46	37	13:30
	F	46	16	15:30
25–29	M	43	34	14:00
	F	43	13	16:08
30–34	M	40	31	14:30
	F	40	11	16:45

Keep in mind, these are the absolute bare-minimum requirements. This is the worst you can do and still pass. If you can do better, by all means, do so. Your goal should be to do better than the last time every time you take a PFA.

Here comes a little tip for when you're running your mile and a half. The tracks in Freedom Hall are not the standard quarter-mile in length. It will take you twelve laps around the track to complete a mile and a half. You will wear a chip on your ankle that will keep track of your time, but you are responsible for keeping count of your laps. It sometimes happens that Recruits count incorrectly and only end up running eleven laps. This invalidates your run and you fail the PFA. Conversely, if you accidentally run an extra lap, it will skew your time to look longer. So, here's the tip. Instead of just counting with numbers when you cross the line, use the months of the year to help you keep track. When you cross the line after one lap around, say January. Next time, February, and so on. Once you've said December, you can stop.

Inspections

Inspections are the bane of a Recruit's existence, and there are several of them that you individually and your division must pass. This is where attention to detail really comes into play in a big way.

Bunk and Locker Inspection. Your first inspection will be of your rack and locker. You will be taught in your first few days of boot camp how to make your bed the proper way (the only way, in other words). This involves smoothing the lumps and wrinkles out of the sheets, folding the top sheet down in a specific way, making 45 degree angle folds in the ends of the sheets where you tuck them under, and even making sure your pillow is in its case and placed on the bed in a specific way. It's ridiculously detailed, and every detail is inspected.

You will also fold and hang your towel a certain way, and hang your Smurf suit to exact specifications. Your tennis shoes will go at one end of your rack, lined up with the wheel, and your boots will go at the other, also precisely aligned.

There is also a particular and rather complicated way of folding the blanket, and the folds have to be a certain size and properly aligned.

I know it sounds ridiculous, and yes, it is a giant pain in the ass to do this stuff every morning, but that's just how it is.

All of this will be inspected, which means that a petty officer or chief with FQA (more on them in a moment) will go over your rack and actually measure stuff with a little ruler. They are looking for any little mistake or imperfection. They are looking for reasons for deduct points from your score. As they go, they will tear up your rack and then you will have to remake it once the inspection is over.

They will also go over the inside of your rack, the locker where all your uniforms and gear are stored. Everything must be properly aligned, put in its proper place in its proper compartment, and folded exactly correctly. If you're not good at folding, get help and practice before the inspection. The inspector will also mess up the locker and throw your stuff around, and you'll have to fix all that later, too.

Inspections also involve a lot of standing at attention, waiting for the inspector to arrive and do their thing. I'm gonna tell you straight up; inspections suck. Some are easier than others, but they all suck to varying degrees. Practicing for inspections also sucks, a lot.

Uniform Inspections. You'll have two uniform inspections, one for your NWU and one for dress and service uniforms (which uniform you are required to wear for this one is the luck of the draw; some people will wear a dress uniform, others will wear the NSU). The inspector will tell you which one.

For the NWU inspection, they'll look at things like how well your sleeves are rolled up, whether your **gig line** is straight, whether your boots are laced correctly and are properly shiny, and whether there are any stray threads sticking out of your buttons or seams.

The NSU and dress inspection is a little more detailed, as the uniforms themselves are a little more complicated and you will have to wear your ribbons. The inspector will take note of how you wear your cover, whether your ribbons are placed correctly, gig line, shoes, gear adrift, etc.

For each of these inspections, you will also have to answer a question. When the inspector comes to you, he or she will ask you a question while they inspect you. This question will probably be on rank recognition, the chain of command, or the general orders. Make sure you've been studying these and can recite them by heart.

Zone Inspection. Zone inspection is a little nerve-wracking because it involves an inspector going over every inch of your living space with a white glove (literally). Everything, and I mean everything, in your compartment must be dusted, shined, folded, smoothed, etc. This includes your rack and locker. It's a real team effort, and they really do go over the compartment with a fine-toothed comb.

Weapon Turnover Inspection. This is probably the most nerve-wracking inspection you'll undergo, simply because there are so many little things that can go wrong.

This inspection is unique because it involves the handling of a weapon. You will be trained in the handling and specifications of a Beretta M9 pistol. It's very regimented and rigorous, meaning you'll be expected to answer questions with an exact, specific answer and perform the turnover in a very specific way come inspection day.

The lead-up to this inspection involves properly donning a holster and lanyard and then standing in ranks at parade rest while the actual turnover takes place.

The process of turning over the weapon, in basic terms, involves loading and unloading the weapon and then handing the weapon over to the person behind you. It sounds simple, but there are very specific steps and ways of performing those steps that you will have to get just right. The process itself is a little too complicated to explain here, and it probably wouldn't make much sense anyway—it's one of those things you have to experience to fully understand—so I will just say that the things you most need to watch out for are: not dropping the bullet, keeping the muzzle of the gun inside the clearing barrel, and absolutely not doing ANYTHING until the inspector says "proceed." And make sure you know the answers to the questions about the weapon and about FPCONs.

After your division passes this inspection, you will start carrying a weapon while on watch.

And just note that these weapons have all been de-militarized; they've had the firing pins removed, so there's no chance that you're going to shoot yourself or anyone else. You will still catch serious shit for pointing it at someone, however.

Drill Inspection. If your division is anything like my division, this is the inspection that will cause the most frustration and require the most practice. You'll need to show that you can march with precision and coordination, stand at attention or parade rest with great patience and military bearing, and properly carry and present your division's flags.

If you're not carrying a flag and you're not the RPOC or AROC, your job is relatively easy. Relatively. You will be responsible for knowing how to march and execute facing movements as part of a formation. If you've never marched before, there's a fairly steep learning curve, especially when you're dealing with a bunch of other people who have never marched before. You may hear the term "clusterfuck" a lot while you're practicing.

The people who do the inspection are experts in drilling. These are the petty officers who run 900 divisions normally. They know what they're looking for.

This inspection is particularly hard on the RPOC and on the flags and the guidon. A lot is riding on their performance, individually and as a group. A good RPOC can save an otherwise mediocre inspection, and a flustered RPOC can bring down a whole division.

This drill routine can seem like a waste of time — how much marching are you going to do in the fleet? — but in fact it is this exact sequence that you will need to execute at graduation, so it is important that you know what you're doing and that you look good doing it so that you can wow the audience on graduation day.

The Perils of FQA. FQA stands for "Fleet Quality Assurance." These are the people that can make your life hell, because even your RDCs live in fear and loathing of them.

If you're going somewhere on your own or as part of a small group unaccompanied by an RDC, you'll need to watch out for these guys. They can pull you over at random and inspect you, and they are not nice about it.

FQA inspectors can also pop into your compartment while your division is out and inspect racks and lockers. This is why RDCs don't like them. They come in unannounced and fuck stuff up and give your division hits while you're not even there to defend yourselves. RDCs also resent the fact that an FQA inspector can halt a whole division and inspect the recruit leaders and yeomen.

The Recruits who have to worry most about the FQA buzzkills, however, are RPOCs and yeomen. Yeomen, make sure you have everything you're supposed to have in that black bag, because FQA likes nothing better than to write yeomen up for forgetting things. And your RDCs will get even with you later. And RPOCs, be on your guard. If an FQA inspector catches you messing up once, they may actually keep an eye out for you in future. RDCs don't like that, and you'll pay for it.

⚓

Battle Stations

What to Expect. Battle Stations and the simulator on which it takes place are treated more or less as big secrets by the Navy. If you Google it, you'll find out that it was designed by Hollywood special effects experts (it's true) and that it cost bajillions of dollars, but you probably won't find much actually useful information. That's because the Navy forbids sailors to give details about what goes on during Battle Stations and about details of the simulator itself.

In this instance, because I swore I wouldn't and because I have a security clearance to maintain, I'm not going to reveal ultra-specific information about Battle Stations. I will tell you as much as I can without saying too much. I'm not going to put myself as a writer or you as a reader in a position where either of us can be accused of cheating on Battle Stations. Cheating or suspected cheating on Battle Stations will land you in big trouble.

So, here's what I can tell you. The USS *Troyer* is shaped like half a ship. It floats in actual water and in every way simulates an actual Navy vessel. The inside is particularly impressive.

Battle Stations involves a series of evolutions over the course of about twelve hours. (It happens overnight). You will run Battle Stations along with several other divisions because the *Troyer* is big enough to fit that many people. You won't have much contact with anyone else, though, except for passing each other in the P-ways. Anyway, you'll break down into groups and everyone in the group will rotate through being the group leader. You'll be the leader for at least one evolution, and you won't know which one in advance, so be ready for anything.

Without giving too much away, I hope, the things you'll have to accomplish may include:

- loading supplies onto the ship,
- handling line,
- standing watch,
- donning protective gear,
- transporting injured shipmates,
- dealing with flooding,
- exiting a smoke-filled compartment,
- and other fun things.

It's a long night. It's physically and mentally tiring. Probably the hardest part is staying awake between evolutions (and you'd better stay awake). Between evolutions, you'll have time to hydrate and take a pee. I really recommend staying well-hydrated for Battle Stations, and don't sit down unless you are told to. If you sit, next thing you know you'll be nodding off.

Anyway, there's no great trick to Battle Stations. Be a team player, keep your mind focused on what you're doing, and play it like a video game. By that, I mean you should look at each evolution as a level. Focus on the level you're on, pass it, and move on to the next. Also, don't goof off. There are petty officers everywhere on the *Troyer*, and they like to see that you're taking Battle Stations seriously.

A petty officer will accompany your group wherever you go. They aren't supposed to offer any help, though some of them do anyway by offering little hints or reminders. Many of these petty officers are really nice and friendly. Others are not. It's a crapshoot. Their job is to monitor your performance and give or take away points. Points are awarded for successful completion of each evolution, as well as for things like teamwork, leadership skills and efficiency. Points are taken away for things like arguing, disorganization, forgetting to turn your air supply on when you put on the oxygen apparatus, etc.

Like I said, there's no real secret or magical trick to passing Battle Stations. Just treat it like you should treat the rest of boot camp; keep calm, focus, listen, and help your team.

Passing and Getting Capped. Do people fail Battle Stations? Yes, they do. But there's really no excuse. As long as you're listening to what you're told and staying focused on what you're doing, you shouldn't have much of a problem. People who fail are the people who fall asleep, who start thinking

too far ahead and get distracted, or who aren't working well with their team. If your monitor tells you
to correct something, do it. Pay attention to detail.
You'll be fine.

I'm going to assume that you're going to pass
Battle Stations, because you are well- prepared and
level-headed, as evidenced by the fact that you are
reading this book. So, once the night is finally over
and you are informed that you have passed, there
will be a ceremony called "capping." This is where
you finally trade that damned "Recruit" cap you've
been wearing for one that says "Navy." It's a small
gesture, but it means a lot.

For most people, this is the most emotional
moment of boot camp. It tends to be even more
emotional than graduation, because it's the moment
when you officially become a United States Sailor,
and pride in yourself and relief that the hardest
part is over will probably come flooding over you. I
never cry. Ask anyone I know. But I cried when I got
capped.

I won't detract from the specialness of the
moment by describing the ceremony in detail, but
just know that it is a big deal and you should be very
proud of yourself for having made it through.

The Aftermath. Once you're back in your ship,
you'll be able to eat a nice meal (go ahead and have
that ice cream or cookie now) and you may find that

you don't really have much to do. This is not an excuse to goof off or fall asleep. If you fall asleep before taps, you're gonna get it. Don't lean on your rack or the bulkhead and don't try to hide in the head and take a nap. Find something to do, like shining your shoes or inspecting your dress uniform for graduation, and make sure there are people around you to wake you up if you start to nod off. Keep each other awake and usefully occupied.

Also, at some point you'll be able to make a phone call home. If you go back to the compartment before phone call time, that's all the more reason to stay awake and on task. Goofing off or napping is a good reason for your RDCs to shorten your phone time.

⚓

Out the Other End

Alright. You've made it through two of the toughest, weirdest months of your life and you are now part of the world's finest navy. You are no longer a Recruit. But wait a minute; don't relax too much. Boot camp isn't quite over yet.

There are no more tests to pass, no PFAs to run. Other Recruits will look up to you with envy. You will feel relieved and proud. But you are still expected to behave in the same formal manner as before. You will not treat your RDCs differently, and they will not treat you differently. Don't lose your military bearing, don't get lazy or complacent and don't assume you can no longer get in trouble. My division got the shit IT'd out of us the night before we left boot camp for letting our discipline and military bearing slip. In other words, go ahead and be proud and relieved, but don't get cocky or lax. The same standards and requirements that have applied throughout boot camp still apply after Battle Stations and even after the graduation ceremony.

Pizza Dinner. After you pass Battle Stations and before you graduate, you'll have a big pizza dinner and there will be officers and mucky-mucks present and everyone will make a big deal of you. Enjoy it, but just a word of caution; don't overindulge. There will be pizza, soda and ice cream, and you should enjoy it because you've earned it. However, your body will not be used to having such greasy or sweet food, and it can be a pretty big shock to your system. The last thing you want to do is spend the night before and morning of graduation puking in the head.

Pride Run. Before you graduate, your division will get to perform what's called the Pride Run. Most of the year, this is done outdoors and involves running around the base with all your flags, chanting and letting everyone know that you're done. I've heard it's pretty cool, but I wouldn't really know because I went in the middle of winter and everything was so icy we had to do our pride run in the gym where no one could see us. Whatever. I'm not bitter.

Captain's Cup. The Captain's Cup is a friendly athletic competition between all the divisions who will be graduating on the same date. It involves things like footraces, pull-up competitions, a stretcher-carrying race, free-throw contests, volleyball, etc. It's a good time and you get to unwind a little and cheer on your shipmates. Everyone can participate in the event of their choice. The division that comes in first overall is awarded with a trophy and a flag to carry at graduation.

Unless things have changed, your division will also come up with a song or chant to perform at the start of Captain's Cup. It's a little corny, but it's fun.

Graduation. The Great Lakes graduation ceremony is a big deal. It involves music and pageantry and speeches from very big people in the Naval hierarchy. Unfortunately for the graduates, it also involves very prolonged periods of standing at attention. Passing out is not uncommon. Just letting you know.

But seriously, graduation is a very cool ceremony and makes you feel like you've really accomplished something (which you have). It's also a pretty emotional day, especially if your family attends (and they really should). How long the ceremony takes depends on how many divisions are graduating that day, but it averages a little over an hour.

You'll be wearing your dress uniform (whites or blues, depending on the season) and that's what you'll wear off-base for your first day of liberty. Graduation takes place at about 0900 in the morning, so as soon as they call "Liberty call, liberty call!" (some of the sweetest words you'll ever hear), you're free to meet up with your family and spend the day in town.

Liberty Weekend. Liberty Weekend is your last weekend at Great Lakes (as long as you're not put on hold for some weird administrative reason, but that's not very common).

Anyway, Liberty Weekend is pretty sweet, but the freedom is only relative. You will wear your peanut butters, you will be expected to maintain military bearing, and you will be responsible for getting back to your ship on time each evening. Your RDCs will determine what time you need to be back. Don't be the asshole who gets the whole division in trouble because you were late. Be early.

If you go to the giant mall in Great Lakes, be aware that that is where all the off-duty RDCs go on the weekend, too. They will be watching you, and you won't even know it. They take great pleasure in reporting to *your* RDCs about how you were picking your nose or talking on your cell phone while walking or eating while walking or wearing your uniform incorrectly or whatever else. Be careful out there.

Even if you are married, you will not be permitted to stay overnight off base. You will also not be allowed to drive. But there's plenty of public transportation available, so don't worry. My advice is to make friends with your initial cab driver and tell him you'd like to use him all weekend. Chances are he'll give you a price break, and you can prearrange where and what time you and your family would like to be picked up each morning.

There will still be a watchbill on liberty weekend. Hopefully, the division you are berthed with will take care of the daytime watches, but it just depends on what they are required to do that day. You may have to stand a watch during the day, so just be ready. More likely, you'll stand watch at night, but either way be prepared for the fact that your regular responsibilities aren't over until the day you leave Great Lakes.

I want to emphasize that, while you are technically free to purchase anything you want while on liberty weekend, don't, under any circumstances and no matter what it is, bring it back on base with you. At best it will be confiscated, and at worst you may find yourself in front of a Captain's Mast. Even though you've graduated, anything you have other than what has been issued to you is still considered contraband. You can leave whatever you buy with your family and they can mail it to you once you get to A-school.

Same goes for cell phones. Cell phones are just as forbidden after graduation as they are before. Don't think you can get away with it. You can't.

Leaving for A-school or the Fleet. Unless you are undesignated, you will be going to A-school immediately after boot camp. If you are undesignated, you'll be heading out to the fleet.

Either way, your new Navy career starts right away. You will not be given leave between boot camp and A-school. If you get to A-school and you have to wait to "class up," which is more than likely, you will not spend that time on leave. You will spend that time on hold, cleaning the barracks every day. The first time you will be able to apply for non-emergency leave is after you graduate A-school. The good news is, A-school is not the isolated little world that boot camp is. You'll be able to go off base on weekends and, after a couple of weeks, during the week after school. Your family can visit you whenever they like, and you can have your cell phone and computer so you can keep in touch.

You'll probably leave Great Lakes for the airport very early in the morning, and then you'll probably have to hang around the airport for quite awhile. It sucks having to lug your seabag and garment bag up to check-in counter, but once you've checked them, it's smooth sailing.

When you get to your A-school, you'll check in and get your room assignment. Then you'll be able to unpack and pretty much do what you like. I recommend finding the computer lab at the MWR area.

A-school uses a phased liberty program. At first, you'll be phase zero, meaning you don't get to go off base except on weekends, and you have to be in uniform even when you do go off base. You'll also have a curfew. The liberty phases gradually get less and less restrictive, so eventually you'll be able to go off base after school hours on weekdays and stay out until pretty late.

⚓

Stuff That Will Get You in Big Trouble

This section is devoted to the things that will get you in guaranteed trouble. By "trouble" I don't just mean getting IT'd or getting screamed at; I mean real trouble. Like, potentially career-ending trouble. As you will probably witness for yourself, these kinds of things happen more than you might think. You will be warned against these things early and often at Great Lakes, but I'm going to give you a preview so you know going in. In no particular order, the main major offenses are:

- **Recruit-to-Recruit contact:** This means touching another Recruit. It's especially egregious when it happens between members of the opposite sex, but it includes any time you place a hand (or other body part) on another Recruit. It includes holding hands, patting on the back, pushing, nudging, etc. This is important to remember: it also includes sending letters to Recruits who are in other divisions or attempting to pass them notes. If you came to boot camp with a friend or loved one and they were placed in a different division than you, be prepared not to have contact with that Recruit until graduation. If you end up in the same room with that person during the course of boot camp and you feel you absolutely must make contact with them, ask your RDC's permission first (and be prepared to be denied).

• **Malingering:** This basically means faking illness or injury. People do this in order to get time off or to avoid doing things they don't feel like doing, like PT, marching, classroom instruction, etc. Your RDCs are not dumb. Chances are, they've been doing their job for awhile. They know the tricks Recruits try to use. If you're malingering, or they suspect you are, or the corpsmen at sick call suspect you are, it's gonna be a very bad day for you. Malingering is punishable under the Uniform Code of Military Justice (UCMJ).

• **Contraband:** Contraband can range from cell phones down to food taken from the galley. Unless they've changed it since I went, you'll be shown actual footage of a Recruit who brought a cell phone back from liberty weekend. She had already graduated, and as punishment she had her pay docked and was set all the way back to P-days! It's not worth it. It's really not. And don't sneak apples and granola bars and stuff out of the galley. It's considered stealing. If you have something you know or suspect you're not supposed to have, come clean. It's not gonna be pretty, but it's better than having someone catch you and rat you out. (There's always someone ready to rat you out).

• **Arguing with an RDC or other person in authority:** Oh my God, please don't do it. There may come a time when you feel you've been treated unfairly, or when your RDCs are just pissing you off in a general way. Don't argue. If you feel you've genuinely been mistreated, there are official channels for addressing those issues. Otherwise, just suck it up. Blowing up at an RDC or getting in their face (or even rolling your eyes) may be treated as another UCMJ-punishable offense, such as refusal to follow a direct order. Keep your temper in check.

• **Fighting and harassment:** This is in the same vein as Recruit-to-Recruit contact, but more serious. Fighting is also punishable under the UCMJ, and depending on the severity of the incident and who's to blame, you could get AS-MO'd or separated from the Navy. Again, keep your temper in check. I know it can be tough, but putting up with assholes builds character, and it's way better than the consequences of putting your hands on another Recruit. Harassment of any kind is absolutely not tolerated. This means name-calling, threats, sexually-suggestive comments or behavior, etc.

Now that you know the major offenses, I'd like to point out that some people take advantage of these things. What I mean by that is that some Recruits decide they don't like certain other Recruits and deliberately set out to get them in as much trouble as possible by accusing them of the above offenses. I saw it happen in my division, and I've heard stories from other people. Be careful, and don't be one of those Recruits.

For Families

Boot camp can be a tough time for those whom the Recruit leaves behind. I've compiled some tips I learned as a Recruit, and I've asked my parents to share some tips, as well. Here goes.

- **Be supportive.** It probably goes without saying, but your Recruit will benefit from your positive attitude about their choice to join the Navy and their upcoming departure for boot camp. If your Recruit feels guilty or sad about leaving, boot camp will be just that much more stressful and difficult for them.

- **Seek support for yourself.** If your son or daughter has never been away from home before, or if your spouse is shipping out to boot camp, you will probably be dealing with a good deal of loneliness and concern for your Recruit's well-being. The loneliness and anxiety are only increased if your Recruit has to spend the holidays at boot camp (like I did). Spending time with family and friends can help a lot, but there are also specific support groups for the families of Sailors and Recruits. Check out navy4moms.com.

- **Send a lot of letters and cards.** This is good for you and a great morale booster for your Recruit. Mail call is a highlight of any day at boot camp, and a letter full of news from home, even just the smallest everyday details, can be a major comfort for a Recruit and a nice time-out from a hectic routine. Be careful, though: you may be tempted to send your Recruit care packages, but restrain yourself. That kind of thing is not allowed at boot camp, and could get your Recruit in pretty big trouble. Don't send food or toiletries. Don't even send books or magazines. You might be able to get away with putting a news clipping or two in a letter or card, but be careful even there. RDCs tend to like to be the ones to give news of the outside world to Recruits, as they see fit, so they may frown upon their Recruits getting clippings. Just stick to regular-old letters and greeting cards (and not the kind of cards that make noises or sing).

• **Don't be discouraged or worried if your Recruit doesn't call you.** Aside from the thirty-second phone call when they arrive and a longer one after Battle Stations, Recruits are not guaranteed any phone calls. Any calls beyond those two are bonuses. How many they get depends largely on the behavior and attitude of their division, and the whim of their RDCs. Not getting a phone call for a long time does not necessarily mean bad news. It may just mean the RDCs feel there isn't time or that the division hasn't done anything extraordinarily deserving of a trip to the phone bank. But rest assured, your Recruit looks forward to being allowed to make phone calls just as much as you do to receiving them. If they are able to, they will call. (It's worth noting that the first time you get a phone call longer than "Hi, I'm here, gotta go," can be pretty emotional for both you and your Recruit. Be prepared for some tears on both sides).

• **If at all possible, attend graduation.** Your Recruit won't have seen you for about two months, and they'll be eager to give you a hug and have you see them on their big day. Boot camp is transformative, even for more mature Recruits who have already had some experience of the world. Your Recruit will have come through a lot and should be proud of themselves. They'll want to show off their new Sailorized self to you and they'll have lots of stories to tell. It's really difficult for new Sailors whose families don't come out for graduation and liberty weekend. They have to watch everyone else hang out with their families, and if they don't have anyone to tag along with, they can't leave base on liberty. Plus, the Great Lakes graduation ceremony is pretty darn cool.

- **Don't put too much weight on what Web sites say about what should be happening when.** The Great Lakes Web site gives a good deal of detail about what happens during each week of boot camp, so you can keep a mental picture of what your Recruit is up to. It's pretty accurate in a generic way, but keep in mind that there is some variation in these things. Some lucky Recruits get put in "push divisions," which are meant to get the Recruit through training in about six weeks instead of the usual eight. This generally happens right before the holidays. On the other hand, other not-so-lucky Recruits go during times when training is scheduled for ten weeks. This usually happens during the holidays. So, while the timeline is a good rough guide, what specific training your Recruit is going through at any given time may be a little different that what's on the generic schedule.

- **Don't stress about your Recruit's well-being, but do encourage your Recruit to be careful.** Accidents and illnesses do happen, but real boot camp is not like the movies (at least not exactly), and it's not like it used to be. Your Recruit will not be smacked around or manhandled by RDCs, and they will not be the victim of a "blanket party" à la *Full Metal Jacket*. There are no live-fire exercises (other than the firing range, where it's impossible to get shot anyway), there is no chance of your Recruit drowning, and medical care is always available for Recruits who get sick or injured. Counseling is also available for those who need it, and each barracks has its own chaplain. Sniffles and the flu are pretty common, but that's nothing that can't be taken care of with a day or two of bed rest and some decongestants. The most common injuries are things like twisted ankles, shin splints and nasty blisters. Recruits who do get injured are not allowed to do any physical activities that might aggravate or worsen the injury. Bottom line, your Recruit will be taken care of should they get sick or injured. If your Recruit's RDCs know that your Recruit is sick or injured, they will not push your Recruit past what is reasonable. Really serious injuries and illnesses are fairly rare at boot camp, but sometimes they can lead to your Recruit being set back if their condition causes them to miss vital training, or to get medically separated from the Navy if it's serious enough. It does happen. However, *probably the leading cause of serious medical conditions at boot camp is not getting treatment soon enough*, and many of the people who get medically separated do so because circumstances cause unreported pre-existing conditions to emerge. Encourage your Recruit to seek medical attention if they are feeling bad or have pain; untreated infections and injuries just get worse in the stressful, physically demanding world of boot camp. If you know your Recruit has a physical or mental condition that they're trying to hide from the Navy, they need to know that boot camp tends to bring those things out and that the consequence will be separation: if not for the condition itself, then for not being honest about it.

• **Know the emergency contact procedure.** While your Recruit is taking a time out from the real world, life at home goes on. Family emergencies happen. Since you will not be allowed direct contact with your Recruit, you must instead go through the Red Cross. Early on, your Recruit will send you a package containing information on graduation and emergency contact procedures. Keep this information. If there is a death or serious illness in the family, you will need to contact the Red Cross at Great Lakes. They will confirm that there is, indeed, an emergency, and they will inform your Recruit's RDCs and probably a chaplain, as well. The RDCs and chaplain will then alert your Recruit. If necessary, arrangements will then be made for your Recruit to be put on emergency leave for a few days so they can go home. The Navy will arrange your Recruit's travel. If the emergency leave granted is for more than three days (which is unlikely) or if it involves your Recruit missing any mandatory training, your Recruit will be set back into another division and will therefore graduate later than originally scheduled.

For Females

The rest of this book can be applied to any Recruit, but as a female you probably have some concerns that apply specifically to you. What happens when you're on your period? What do you do with your hair? What about birth control and female health issues? Well, fortunately for you, I am a female myself and can address these issues from personal experience.

Your Period. Boot camp is about two months long, so you may expect to get your period twice while you're there. However, as you may already have experienced, your period can be a fickle thing and is easily influenced by things like changes in diet and exercise, being in a different time zone, and living in close quarters with other females. This may mean that you have your period more often, or it may mean that it happens later or even not at all. Personally, I had just finished my period when I arrived at boot camp, and didn't have it the next month. It was kind of a relief, because it was one less thing to deal with.

Now, if you do still experience your period while at boot camp, it's not that big a deal. It's a little inconvenient, but when is it not? On your division's first trip to the store, the females will probably be instructed to buy one or two packages of pads or tampons each. Get whatever brand you prefer, but keep in mind that these will not be for your exclusive use. They will get put into a cabinet in the head and become communal property, so if your brand runs out, you may have to switch temporarily and use whatever is available.

While you're hanging around the compartment, being on your period isn't really an inconvenience, because you can go to the head whenever you need. It's when your division is out and about that things can get a little funky. As I mentioned in an earlier section, you're not allowed to carry anything in your pockets, so you can't just pop a couple of pads into your pockets and relax. No, your yeoman will be responsible for carrying a few pads and tampons in their bag at all times.. If your division is out doing something and you need to change your tampon or pad, you'll have to ask your yeoman for one. You just better hope that your yeoman doesn't forget to stock up regularly or you may be in a messy situation, literally.

And if you're on your period when the swim test rolls around ... well, I hope you use tampons. Otherwise, it could get a little awkward.

And yes, having to shower communally while you're on your period kind of sucks. It also sucks having to use a white towel. And we all know that occasionally, a little leakage happens and underwear and perhaps even sheets fall victim. Fortunately, your laundry PO and your female RDC know that, too. If you have to change your sheets before the next scheduled change, let your female RDC know and she'll help you out. It may be a little embarrassing, but it happens and all females understand. You will not get ridiculed or reprimanded.

Birth Control. You will be given an opportunity to go on one of several types of birth control while at boot camp. This is great if you're currently on the pill and don't want to interrupt the cycle for two months. However, it can also be a real boon even if you're not currently on any type of contraceptive, because it may help keep you from getting your period and you can hopefully avoid the situations described above.

Birth control will be made available to you in the form of the pill, an implant in your arm or a uterine device. The choice is yours. The pill has the advantages of being non-invasive and easily reversible. The other two, while they require a procedure to put in place, are a good choice if you plan to continue using birth control after boot camp but don't want to be bothered with keeping up with pills. They will all be explained in more depth when your division visits *Red Rover*.

The Female Exam. You will be given a pelvic exam at *Red Rover*. It sucks, but it's hardly the end of the world. It will be performed by an actual Navy doctor (an officer) and not by just another corpsman, so that's a good thing. I can't guarantee that your doctor will be female, but mine was, and I think Great Lakes makes an effort to have female doctors perform these exams. There may be a male assistant present, however.

If you've never had one of these exams before, you may be freaking out a little. Seriously, don't worry about it. I'm not going to lie and tell you it doesn't hurt. It does. There's nothing particularly pleasant about having your vajayjay opened way beyond normal with a metal implement. But it's over in about five minutes. And honestly, it's really not embarrassing. You think it's going to be embarrassing, but then you get up on the table and the doctor does her thing and you realize that this is what she does pretty much all day. It's totally routine and no one's looking at you with judgement or anything else beyond clinical evaluation. All in all, it's an uncomfortable situation that lasts about ten minutes total, and then you're done and you move on with your day.

Your doctor will also perform a manual breast check on you, and she'll go over the importance of calcium intake. She'll probably recommend that you drink a couple of glasses of milk at the galley every day, and she may even give you a bottle of calcium pills, depending on your dietary habits. Boot camp is not the place for brittle bones.

Hair and Beauty. Forget it.

Even if you had a decent haircut, which you almost certainly won't, there's really not much you can do with your hair at boot camp. Pony tails are not in regulation and your hair won't be long enough for a bun. Even if it were, you're not going to have access to any kind of hair tie beyond little metal or plastic clips. My female RDC allowed us to wear two clips, port and starboard, and that was it. How many clips you're allowed and where you can place them is up to your female RDC, but I'm telling you right now, abandon all thought of looking cute. Without any kind of product or accessory or access to a hair dryer, there's just not much that can be done with bob-length hair. Plus, you'll be wearing a hat much of the time, and we all know what that does to hair. Permanent helmet head. I got to the point where I would see myself in the mirror in the morning, shrug and walk away. No one looks good, so no one really cares what you look like. You'll be expected to keep your hair reasonably neat and out of your face, and that's about all you can aim for.

It is highly unlikely that you will be allowed to pluck or otherwise maintain your eyebrows until liberty weekend. To be perfectly honest, I sneaked a quick swipe of my razor at my eyebrow area once or twice out of sheer desperation, but our RDCs had warned us not to do anything to our eyebrows or we'd be in trouble if they noticed. That was the only reason I was grateful for those huge glasses; no one could see my eyebrows too much.

As for shaving, that will likely only happen once a week, on Sundays, when you can spend a little more time in the shower. There just won't be enough time otherwise.

It should go without saying that there are no cosmetics allowed at boot camp. Don't bring any from home, because they will end up in the trash. You may be allowed to purchase some makeup at the NEX before you have your pictures taken. Picture day and graduation will be the only days you are allowed to wear it, and you should expect your RDCs to inspect your face to make sure you haven't overdone it. You can also wear makeup on liberty weekend, but again, don't overdo it, because you will be in uniform and will need to be in regulations. Also, if you buy any makeup (or anything else for that matter) while on liberty, don't bring it back to the compartment. Send it home with your family and they can mail it out to you at A-school.

Once you get out to the real Navy, you can wear your hair down if it's short enough or in a bun, and you can wear tasteful amounts of makeup and jewelry. Just tough it out for two months and you'll be okay.

Getting ASMO'd or Separated

Okay, before you start getting nervous, let me say that getting set back or failing out isn't too likely to happen to you, and there are a lot of things you can do to avoid those fates. But it does happen, and I can virtually guarantee that one or the other will happen to at least one person in your division. This section is about what getting ASMO'd or separated entail, why it happens, and some of the ways you can keep them from happening to you.

ASMO stands for "assignment memorandum orders," and it's the term for getting set back. This involves getting put into a different division that is a little bit behind the timeline of your original division, usually two weeks. Generally, when a Recruit gets ASMO'd it's for not passing requirements. For example, if you don't pass one of the academic tests, you'll get set back a couple of weeks into a division that has not taken that test yet, so you can take it again. Or, if you don't pass the swim by the time your division runs Battle Stations, you'll get set back to give you a couple of extra weeks to pass it. It is also possible, though rare, to get ASMO'd for disciplinary reasons. If you're a troublemaker and your RDCs are tired of dealing with you, they can set you back as far as they want. Therefore, it is possible to be within days of graduating and get set back to P-days for

disciplinary reasons. It is also possible to get AS-
MO'd after you graduate, for example if you screw up
over liberty weekend. That will most likely involve a
Captain's Mast.

Separation means that you are kicked out of the
Navy entirely. Separation for disciplinary reasons is
rare. The offense would have to be pretty egregious.
However, separation for medical reasons does happen to a relatively small but still significant number
of Recruits. This mostly happens to people who
come in with an unreported pre-existing condition
which then worsens. We had several people from my
division separated for medical reasons within the
first two or three weeks. One had a heart condition,
one had a joint condition and another fainted in
the head from not eating for days. Similarly, a small
handful of Recruits have mental conditions they
don't report which then come out in the stressful environment of boot camp. Some just find boot camp
to be too much, and they snap. They sleepwalk or pee
the bed or just wig out. These people are rare, and
they should know better than to enlist in the first
place, but they're out there.

People who end up getting separated for mental or physical problems don't go home immediately. They usually spend at least a couple of weeks in
Ship 5, being evaluated and monitored. (Parents, if
you get a call saying your Recruit is in Ship 5, that's

not good news.) My point here is that if you decide the Navy isn't for you and you fake or exaggerate a condition to get out, your exit will be anything but speedy. In fact, you may be there longer than it would take for you to graduate under normal circumstances. I've heard rumors of people (very rare cases) being kept in Ship 5 for up to a year. *The fastest way out of boot camp is graduation.*

How to Avoid Getting ASMO'd or Separated. As I mentioned, most ASMOs happen for failing to meet requirements in a timely manner. The solution, therefore, is to do your very best to pass your requirements. Study hard for tests. You will get two chances to pass each academic test, and after that comes the ASMO. So, if you don't pass the first time, really buckle down the second time. Find someone who did well and ask them to be your study partner. Failing the swim test is a big reason for getting ASMO'd, but you will have your entire time at boot camp up until Battle Stations to try to pass it. If you don't pass it the first time, you'll take it again every day until you do. I know of a couple of people who didn't pass the swim until the night before Battle Stations. Not an ideal situation, but they did graduate on time.

Also, if you don't pass your final PFA, you'll get ASMO'd. Three people from my division didn't graduate with us because they didn't pass their final run. If you get ASMO'd because of the PFA, you'll be placed in the world's saddest unit, FEP (Fitness and Exercise Program). This is a division which literally does nothing but train for and repeatedly take the PFA. You will remain in FEP until one of two things happens: you pass the PFA and graduate; or, more likely, you break, physically or mentally, and get separated from the service. Very few Recruits graduate from FEP. They either get so physically worn out that they get badly injured, or they give in to the prevailing attitude of desperation and hopelessness and have a mental breakdown or just quit. Hence my emphasis on being able to run.

Another great way to avoid being ASMO'd is to behave yourself. Follow the rules, keep your hands off other Recruits, and don't argue with the RDCs and you should be okay.

To help avoid getting separated for mental or physical reasons, the best tip I can give you is simply this: If you know you have a condition that might even possibly rear its head at boot camp or in the fleet, don't join the Navy. If it's too late and you already signed on the dotted line, this may be a good time to tell your recruiter you're hiding something. Yes, that means you signed up under false pretenses, and you may get in trouble, but it's better than getting to boot camp, getting irreversibly injured or suffering a mental breakdown, and then having to spend weeks or months being monitored in Ship 5 before being separated from the service with no hope of ever being able to enlist again. Save yourself a few steps and come clean now.

Glossary

A-school: The job-specific training course you will attend immediately after boot camp.

ASMO: Assignment Memorandum Orders. Pronounced "azmo." The term for being set back in your progress for failure to meet requirements or for disciplinary reasons.

blouse: Uniform shirt. You will wear a t-shirt as an undershirt and the shirt you wear on top is the blouse (even for males).

bulkhead: Wall. Don't lean on the bulkheads.

Captain's Mast: A non-judicial proceeding, less severe than a court-martial. Held for Recruits and Sailors who find themselves in violation of Navy or military laws and regulations. A superior officer, generally a captain, will act as judge and jury.

chest candy: Ribbons worn on the blouse. Ribbons and medals are awarded for achievements or conduct. At boot camp, you will have the chance to earn chest candy in the form of a pistol qualification.

chow: Any meal. There is no "food" in the Navy, nor are there "breakfast," "lunch," or "dinner;" it's all chow.

cover: Hat. Also the command for putting on your hat ("uncover" is the command for taking your hat off). If you are wearing a cover, you are said to be "covered;" when not wearing a cover, you are "uncovered."

deck: The floor.

evolution: Any scheduled activity. Your first evolution may be chow and the next may be class-room instruction.

FFD: "Fit for Full Duty." Judged physically able to perform all necessary tasks.

galley: Dining hall, cafeteria.

gig line: The line formed by the buttons of your blouse and the fly of your pants. You will be taught exactly where it is and how to keep it straight.

head: The bathroom, or a toilet itself.

height-line: A single-file line in which Recruits are arranged in order of height, shortest to tallest.

hygiene: To take a shower.

inboard: Towards the middle of the room. Your boots go on the inboard side of your rack.

inter-station pass: Basically a version of the hall pass you carried in elementary school. A signed form saying you have permission from someone in authority (usually and RDC) to transit to a specified destination. Used when transiting alone or as a small group. You will carry a blank one in your blouse pocket at all times, just in case.

knit bag: A little mesh bag with a zipper. You'll be issued several of these. Mainly, you'll use them for putting your socks and skivvies in for laundering, so they don't get lost.

LLD: "Light Limited Duty." The status you are given when you have an injury and are not able to do all the physical things you would normally be required to do.

outboard: Towards the edge of the compartment. Your tennis shoes go under the outboard side of your rack.

P-way: Short for "passageway." A hallway.

port: Left-hand side.

quarterdeck: Basically, the main entry and exit point from a ship.

Recruit handwriting: Block, all-capital-letter handwriting, the exclusive type of writing you will use at boot camp. It must be neat and precise. There are posters of proper Recruit handwriting form all over the place.

reveille: Wake-up time. Also known as "rev," which can be used as a verb, as in, "We revved at 0500 this morning."

running lights: Red lights that are turned on after taps. These are used so that watchstanders can see what they are doing, without ruining their night vision or disturbing the sleep of others.

scuttlebutt: A drinking fountain. Also, more rarely, gossip or rumors.

secure: To stop, end, forbid, or put away. Walking is secured in Freedom Hall; you will jog everywhere. If dessert is secured by your RDCs, you better not get caught having a cookie. When field day is over, word will be passed that field day is secured. If it's warm, parkas will be secured.

starboard: Right-hand side.

swab: Mop, used as a noun or verb. You swab the deck with a swab.

taps: Bedtime. Can be used a verb, as in, "What time do we tap tonight?"

www.ingramcontent.com/pod-product-compliance
Lightning Source LLC
Chambersburg PA
CBHW072128280526
45788CB00002B/579